Design Wise

*A guide for evaluating the
interface design of
information resources*

by Alison J. Head

CyberAge Books

Information Today, Inc.
Medford, New Jersey

3/2/01

Second Printing, 2000

Design Wise: A Guide for Evaluating the Interface Design of Information Resources

Library of Congress Cataloging-in-Publication Data
Head, Alison J., 1957–
    Design wise : a guide for evaluating the interface design of information resources / by Alison J. Head.
        p.   cm.
    Includes bibliographical references and index.
    ISBN 0-910965-39-0 (hardcover)   ISBN 0-910965-31-5 (paperback)
    1. Human-computer interaction.   2. User interfaces (Computer systems)   I. Title.
    QA76.9.H85H42   1999
    004'.01'9—dc21   98-43724
                                                                              CIP

Printed and bound in the United States of America.

Cover Design: Bette Tumasz
Book Design: Trejo Production, Princeton, NJ
Chart Design: Therese Bettinelli
Copy Editor: Michelle Sutton-Kerchner
Editor in Chief: John B. Bryans
Publisher: Thomas H. Hogan Sr.

Contents

List of Figures and Tables

Foreword

I had the pleasure and the terror of meeting Alison Head in 1997, when she sat in on my interactive media class at Stanford University. The pleasure was in making contact with another human who actually understood what I was talking about when I'd make my pronouncements about interactive design.

The terror, of course, was for the same reason: Alison understood my axioms because she was (and continues to be) the real thing—both a real professor and a real designer of information. By the time we finished our first conversation after the first class meeting ended, it was perfectly obvious that she had a far deeper knowledge of interactive media than I had, even though I've been chronicling the progress of the nascent media form since its inception in the mid-1980s.

The book you're holding is proof that I was right. In *Design Wise*, Alison Head has managed to wrap her arms around one of the most powerful, complex, cross-disciplinary tasks of our digital age: understanding and designing interactive media. Drawing its lessons from years of research in the many disciplines that comprise the study of human-computer interaction, this book demystifies both the conceptual foundation and the practical application of this new media form.

In other words: *Design Wise* doesn't just tell you how, it also tells you why.

Head's fundamental premise, evidenced by the book's title, is that design and utility are inextricably "intertwingled," to borrow the perfect word from technology visionary Ted Nelson (who also invented the term "hypertext" more than thirty years ago, to describe what we now do every time we click a computer mouse to navigate a screen of information). The very best and most sophisticated digital tools in the world can't create good interactive media unless those wielding the tools understand what they're actually trying to accomplish—including the interplay of the many forces that result when human meets machine.

Until now, it has been painfully obvious that achieving a positive result at that meeting has been much easier said than done. Anyone who's tried to click his or her way around a labyrinthine Web site, or tried to forge a path through an inscrutable CD-ROM, could easily conclude that the new and much vaunted information age, with all its promise, could not possibly be for them. After one or two rounds of trying to wrest some information or response out of the blasted things, people are far too often convinced that they are too old fashioned or dumb to ever "get it."

But *Design Wise* shows us that these difficulties are not, in fact, evidence of biological determinism.

The book signals two critical and welcome trends: One is that people like Alison Head exist—people who deeply understand the real and unique issues that arise when we use technology to connect people with the tidal waves of information they generate. The other is that such understanding can not only be made practical, but can be taught.

It's not that many excellent books haven't been written about the singularity of the human-computer interface, books that cover an enormous breadth of research and experience. They range in focus from historical and literary meditations, such as Steven Johnson's remarkable *Interface Culture*, to Terry Winograd and Fernando Flores's pioneering work, *Understanding Computers and Cognition: A New Foundation for Design* and Brenda Laurel's *Computers as Theatre*.

But *Design Wise* is the first book I've seen that takes the lessons of history and the results of this multidisciplinary research, and transforms them into a primer that allows new media designers to begin the creative process from a foundation that's both rich in fundamentals and utilitarian at its core.

By outlining and analyzing the various critical components of interactive media, including interface basics, design, and technology, as well as providing a generous helping of resources, reference materials, and interviews with design and industry leaders, *Design Wise* gives newcomers the chance to learn at the feet of the masters—often and most valuably, from the mistakes they have made over the past decade.

These mistakes, and our continued ignorance of them, has plagued information-age visionaries for decades. During a Stanford University conference in December 1998, Nelson—the aforementioned hypertext visionary—delivered his low, yet well-deserved, opinion of the dismal state of the interactive arts.

Software and interactive media should really be considered a branch of movie making, said Nelson. "We should be studying H. G. Wells and Alfred Hitchcock and the best documentaries" to design them.

The reason is quite simple: Directors don't have to know how a camera works in order to get the emotional response they want from the audience. But for the most part, it is still the camera operators—the programmers and graphic designers—who are performing the functional equivalents of calling the shots and running the editing suites in today's software industry.

The great contribution that a book like *Design Wise* will make is to help spawn a new generation of software directors in Nelson's sense of the term— auteurs who understand interactive media deep in their bones and know how to create a meaningful, useful interactive experience.

—Denise Caruso

Denise Caruso writes the Digital Commerce column for The New York Times.

Preface

As we walked toward the lobby, Don Norman said something that flabbergasted me. At the completion of the interview that appears in chapter 1 of this book, he told me that he wrote his classic book, *The Design of Everyday Things*, in three short months. I stopped with the force of my English Pointer at the threshold of her veterinarian's door. Only three months?!! How could he have possibly accomplished that? But Norman quickly pulled me from my stunned state. He explained that he had actually ruminated for five years on many ideas that became central to the book's content. Essentially, he wrote the book in his mind. For him, writing the book was the process of pulling all of his disparate thoughts together, organizing them, and finally putting them down on paper.

I will confess that *Design Wise* took me longer than three months to write. The thoughts expressed in this book came to me, as Norman's did to him, from seemingly unrelated ideas gained from a combination of sources, including course work, teaching, and practical work experience. My ideas came together and became the basis for a book in 1996 when I took a professional leave from working and teaching to study Human-Computer Interaction (HCI) at Stanford University.

In layperson's terms, HCI is the study of designing usable computer systems for everyday users. If HCI had been around when I was an undergraduate, I would have undoubtedly avoided it with white-knuckled fear. But years later, what I found lurking on the leading edge of computer science curriculum was invaluable to my own work. What I learned in the year at Stanford illuminated my earlier study of information-seeking behavior seven years before as a doctoral student in library and information science at the University of California at Berkeley. The course work at Stanford also directly tied into my work as the director of information management at *The Press Democrat*, a Santa Rosa, California, newspaper owned by *The New York Times*. Part of my job at the paper dealt with picking the *right* computer resources for reporters and editors so that they could better carry out information gathering. Another part of my work involved participation on a Web design team, developing niche publications for the paper's main site. To these endeavors, HCI held an important key.

As I attended classes, in the company of many young students who wanted to develop computer products, I realized that design was an incredible evaluation tool. At the time, I was struck by the idea that knowing about making a well-designed tool was an integral part of making better choices about existing computer resources. When I returned from my leave, I taught a seminar on the basics of interface design to information science graduate students at San Jose State University. I figured that if I could explain the ideas to these students, the book was a real possibility. The teaching experience proved to be richer than I could have ever imagined. I realized that interface design has relevance far beyond the practicalities of building systems. The confirmation led to writing *Design Wise*, in which evaluation and interface design are combined in hopes of expanding approaches to choosing information resources for computers and, ultimately, to provide users with more satisfying tools for their daily work.

—*Alison J. Head*
alison@sonic.net
Sonoma, California

Acknowledgments

Books, in general, are products of busy minds and undying cooperation. This book project has been no exception. Without the help of committed supporters in both my professional and personal life, it is safe to say that *Design Wise* would have never been completed. Some of my greatest thanks go to the four graduate students from San Jose State University's Graduate School of Library and Information Science—Jo Falcon, Elisabeth Green, Enid Irwin, and Meri Rada—who helped me work out the design template that appears at the end of chapter 3 and carried out a lot of the research contained in part 2: Interface Design Analyses. Long after the semester ended, the students generously carried out and wrote up the field tests that appear in part 2. Throughout the entire book-writing experience, the students' comments, critiques, ideas, and excitement made for a more complete book and engaging project.

There are also special thanks to the interviewees who appear at the end of each chapter—Don Norman, Jakob Nielsen, Reva Basch, Péter Jacsó, Lou Rosenfeld, and Anne Mintz—who generously gave of their time, thoughts, opinions, and ideas about what the future might hold. There are thanks for those peers, who prodded, poked, and reviewed the book's content as it was unwinding, offering invaluable hands-on advice and read-throughs, especially my editors Diane Holt and Jill Hunting Boeve and my academic colleagues Bill Fisher and Stuart Sutton. Friends who regularly use computers in their work added helpful comments along the way too, especially Vonnie Matthews, Chris Orr, David Silcox, and Mary Stephens And there is thanks to Tom Wasow, the department chairman of Stanford's symbolic systems, who granted me a visiting scholar position to come study on the campus for a year, which ultimately led to writing this book.

Design Wise would have never materialized without the work of a dedicated production team. John Bryans, the Editor in Chief at Information Today, Inc., took a special interest in this project, shepherding the manuscript through with a watchful eye. Dorothy Pike, the managing editor for books at Information Today, Inc., spent countless hours bringing the text to its publishable form. Therese Bettinelli, a local graphic artist, designed the book's figures that appear in chapter 3.

Finally, beyond this project, there are several people whom I owe particular debt for their ongoing support. My father, Don Head, has never owned a computer and would not know a "back button" from a mouse but is still one of the smartest people I know. My friend and favorite professor, Frances Van Loo, first served on my dissertation committee at Berkeley almost a decade ago and has always rallied me to be my best and to make good. And finally, my husband, Mark Pollock, for his analytical mind, his endless support, his unbridled enthusiasm, and the willingness to share them all.

Introduction

Design Wise is about making better choices. In particular, it is a book for readers who regularly make competitive decisions about which computer-based information resources to use, to purchase, and to recommend to others. You may be a researcher, librarian, technologist, designer, student, or anyone else who is interested in using computer resources for finding information. Whatever the case, you most likely are someone who regularly grapples with making the best choices for resources that are used for information gathering. In these pages, basics from two different fields, evaluation and interface design, are combined and interwoven into a practical handbook that is written from the user perspective. The purpose of *Design Wise* is to go beyond the typical considerations that often sway us into making a choice—like price, availability, or content—so that the design of an interface itself is also a basis for evaluation.

Some Basic Definitions

There are three terms—*information resource, evaluation*, and *interface*—that appear throughout this book. If a resource's primary purpose is to inform or to educate users via a computer system of some sort, it qualifies as an *information resource*. The Centers for Disease Control and Prevention's Web site, for instance, is a computer-based information resource. An online commercial database chock-full of newspaper content is another. A CD-ROM providing facts and photos about every dog breed imaginable is yet another. All of these products or services have something in common. They have been developed for the purpose of organizing and communicating facts, data, information, and knowledge to a set of users performing information retrieval tasks. The topic of this book concerns information resources for computer users, especially the media of CD-ROMs, Web sites, and online commercial providers (like Dialog or Dow Jones).

By *evaluation*, we mean a method of critical assessment and decision making that happens when money is limited and resources are competitively sought out. In many cases, this kind of evaluation occurs in the workplace. In order to obtain anything, a request—either verbal or written—needs to be carefully crafted. Typically, a thorough proposal defines a product and the need for it, compares the product against alternative solutions, weighs advantages and disadvantages, and justifies a final selection. But evaluation takes more than being a strong writer and a fast talker. Whether it is formal or informal, evaluation requires asking all of the right questions at the right time and knowing the answers to expect. To help readers carry out the evaluation process, we have developed a design evaluation template in chapter 3 that is a guide for critically assessing the interface design of any computer-based information resource. The template has questions readers should ask about whether a resource supports users' primary tasks, has an ease of use, and is aesthetically pleasing.

The other term used in these pages, *interface*, refers to how a tangible resource communicates to users through its design. For all practical purposes, an interface is what we see on our end as the user, the visible piece of a system that bundles together all of a system's (or program's) invisible functionalities and operations. An interface is the piece that connects a user and a machine. Typically, a computer interface consists of the screen, what we see on it (icons and menus), and what we use to interact with the system (a mouse or touch screen). When interface designers are developing a product, they make conscious choices about what interface elements to use, how to present them, how they will work, and what trade-offs are optimal. The outcome of this process largely determines an interface's design. All of this matters to users because well-designed resources increase levels of acceptance, learning, use, and satisfaction. At the same time, a well-designed resource reduces the need for ongoing training, as well as reducing fatigue, frustration, and the time it takes to get tasks done.

This Book's Approach

One of the most important questions to ask when evaluating information resources for computers is how interface design affects users' interactions. This line of questioning should, but does not always, enter into the regular evaluation process. We address four main aspects of the design evaluation process and ask:

1. Why does interface design matter to computer users?

2. How does interface design affect computer users and the work they need to accomplish?

3. Which interface design components are important to know about when it comes to judging different information resources?

4. How do field practitioners and research findings describe what makes for good interface design versus bad design?

There are plenty of good books that are broadly related to what is discussed in these pages. Some are buying guides, some are system analysis planning books, and others are interface design handbooks. In most cases, buying guides offer mini reviews of certain products, with content that is soon outdated. System analysis deals with acquisition, implementation, and training issues that are especially useful when carrying out large automation projects but are of limited help in the everyday evaluation of interfaces.

Interface design books deal with learning about how people interact with computer systems, but they are more focused on how better systems can be built. *Design Wise* is different. This book is written from the user's perspective and evaluates how interface design affects daily interaction with resources.

Part 1

This book is divided into two parts. Part 1 is a primer, introducing readers to interface design ideas and resource evaluation techniques. Chapter 1 provides a practical discussion about why and how interface design matters to computer users. We conclude that when computer resources are unintuitive, slow, and frustrating—whether we acknowledge it or not—interface design matters very much to us. Poor design keeps us from the work we need to accomplish. In the end, design matters because it determines whether a tool will ever get used. Much of our design discussion is drawn from the field of Human-Computer Interaction (HCI), which is also defined in this chapter. Don Norman, a leading HCI researcher and author, is interviewed, and he defines what interface design is, explaining how users' expectations of systems have increased.

At first, chapter 2 may confirm many readers' worst suspicions. Mitchell Kapor, the founder of Lotus, tells us in his "Software Design Manifesto" that many in the software industry knowingly design poor products. He calls this the industry's "secret shame." Kapor argues for a change toward ensuring design quality.

This chapter focuses on the way products are developed and interfaces are designed. We present a history of interface design approaches from the waterfall method used to engineer products in the 1970s to the changes that led up to user-centered design, first developed at Xerox Palo Alto Research Center (PARC) during the 1980s on the Star project. The purpose of chapter 2 is to give readers insight into how resources are built—the design trade-offs developers continually face and the quest for seemingly elusive user-centered design practices. The chapter concludes with an interview with Jakob Nielsen, a leading usability engineer and author, who discusses what usability testing is and why it is an increasingly important factor in product development.

Chapter 3 argues that evaluation of computer-based information resources has become more complex than it was before. Much of this transformation has been brought on by the Web. There are more computer information resources for an ever-widening and diverse user base. So far, information-intensive companies have responded to these demands for information by recycling their content into a range of multimedia formats, including CDs and Web sites. As a result, the usual criteria for evaluation— price, content, and availability—may be more obscured these days by a competitive, product-happy market. Information resources for computer users now need to be evaluated on what it is like to use them—or from an interface design perspective.

To orient readers to the questions they need to ask during a design evaluation, an evaluation template for use in the field is provided. To sharpen the focus of the template, I enlisted the aid of four of the brightest graduate students I know from San Jose State University's School of Library and Information Science as research assistants: Jo Falcon, Elisabeth Green, Enid Irwin, and Meri Rada. During a semester-long project, we grappled with fashioning a design evaluation guide that is written *by users and is for users.* Our goal was to develop a template that has wide applicability for readers who want to improve their skills of design evaluation. Chapter 3 concludes with an interview with Reva Basch, a well-known information industry expert and author, who talks about how the evaluation of resources has changed.

Part 2

Part 2 puts the basics of the design template to work by offering three design analyses of everyday information resources for computers. The reviewed resources that make up the chapters are CDs, Web sites, and online commercial providers (e.g., Dialog and Nexis). Within the Web chapter, there is a section about interface design for people with special needs, an often-neglected topic. Each chapter introduces unique design issues that are germane to the resources and that evaluators should be well aware of before they make choices. Each chapter has a "Design in a Nutshell" section, which is a summary of key issues and a "Design Analysis," which more fully discusses research findings and consequences of the medium's design style.

In particular, chapter 4 questions whether CD-ROMs' interface design really delivers ease of use. In the chapter's interview, Péter Jacsó, a columnist and information science professor, discusses the future of CD-ROMs and whether the resources will be eclipsed by the Web. Chapter 5 examines how Web design, still in its infancy, will need to incorporate a more usable design to meet Web users' growing demand for more effective information retrieval techniques. The chapter's interview is with Lou Rosenfeld, the co-author of *Information Architecture for the World Wide Web*, who explains the difficulties of designing information retrieval systems in the less-than heterogeneous Web environment. Chapter 6 weighs the pros and cons of many commercial online services' migration to the Web. In the chapter's closing interview, Anne Mintz, the Director of Information Services at Forbes Inc., talks about how power searchers' research needs differ from end users' needs and why design features matter in supporting each group's tasks.

In general, the purpose of each chapter's design analysis is to provide readers with a synthesis of design-specific research findings about resources and their ability to deliver task support, usability, and aesthetics to users. Each chapter draws from an extensive review across computing and library and information science literature. In this book, key comments, findings, and design issues were extrapolated from sources, critically evaluated for accuracy and relevance, and synthesized to form each chapter's framework. The research assistants and I canvassed both online and off-line resources, specifically checking the literature of product reviews, educational resources, computer science and HCI, library and information science, product reviews, newspapers, and magazines for design-specific comments.

Our search strategy was intentionally broad. We pulled documents from books, journals, Web sites, online providers, live sources, newsletters, and online discussion groups—anything we could get our hands on—looking for pieces and/or comments that identified significant design issues. Finally, we culled through our research findings and looked for patterns among the comments, and then, in most cases, went back to the research process again to refine our search to see if we had missed anything. Additionally, the students field-tested the literature's observations and findings about each medium's design. A field test of a well-known information product appears as a sidebar in each of the design analyses chapters. From a researcher's point of view, our investigation had its share of challenges, surprises, and informational nuggets. At the end of each chapter, we include recommended readings and a design evaluation checklist based on what we consider to be of the greatest importance during an evaluation process.

Predictions

The final pages of this book offer four predictions about the future of information resources, which came about as a by-product of the book-writing process. The predictions are based on four questions about the future of information resources: (1) Where will new information resources come from and who will be the product development leaders and why?; (2) Will agents deliver the information filtering services that users are anxiously anticipating?; (3) How and why will current Web search engines morph to meet users' information retrieval needs?; and (4) What will be the new career path for information professionals? More than anything, what is presented in this closing chapter are emerging developments that readers should closely watch.

Why a Book?

Why are these ideas compiled in a book? Why not a CD or a Web site? The answer is that books still have advantages over other media. In particular, books are still more accessible, more portable, and easier on the eyes for reading than computer screens. It is hoped that many pages of *Design Wise* will end up underlined and dog-eared, sitting near the computer where you regularly use the Web or tucked under your arm when you go out and test new resources for computers. In particular, we expect readers to turn to this book in the following situations:

- A committee on redesigning an intranet seeks comments about the site's "look and feel"

- A Web site that is easy to use for researching financial trends needs to be chosen

- A funding proposal for a certain collection of CDs needs to be written

- A sight-impaired colleague needs an information resource on the Web that is usable

- A recommendation for an online commercial service is sought

The Point

The foundation of this book is the study of how people interact with interfaces when completing information retrieval tasks. More formally, this idea comes from a relatively new field called HCI, which is the study of behavioral aspects of user interactions with computers and methodologies for building more user-centered products. In the past ten years, HCI has become part and parcel of software designers' training curriculum. But knowing how to size up a user-centered design is increasingly as important for people who choose and use tools as it is for those who design them. The design evaluation template presented in this book is for practical use in the field. The design analyses identify key design issues about each resource. Together, the template and the analyses provide the framework readers need to understand design evaluation. Overall, this book contends that an appreciation for robust interface design should be integrally tied to what we trade cash for, trundle back in our arms, and fire-up for everyone else to use—in settings of all kinds and of all sizes.

Part 1

INTERFACE DESIGN BASICS

1

Why Design Matters

It has happened more than once. I run across some souped-up Web version of one of my favorite information sources and, within seconds, I am sucked in. At last, all of that coveted information is compiled in one searchable multimedia extravaganza. With a slight tap to the keyboard, information comes pouring onto the screen like floodwaters from a Midwestern storm. I dive in with careless disregard: hook, line, and online registration. But after a few encounters, my enthusiasm dampens. The site is not all it is cracked up to be. The frenetic graphic that dances across the screen every time I pull up the site begins to annoy me. The circuitous layout wears me out. Searching is slow and frustrating. It does not take long. Less than three months later, I have pulled the site from my bookmark list. Another misbegotten venture in the online world.

Whatever system we are using—whether it is a CD or an online service or a Web site—most of us begin taking an interest in interface design (whether we call it that or not) when aspects of the interface stop working well for us. It is absolutely true that no one likes a slow, plodding CD-ROM. An online service glutted with overwhelmingly bright colors that draws our attention in ninety different directions can be tough to take, too. A Web site with undersized and incomprehensible icons is just plain unnavigable. When an interface becomes clunky, illogical, muddled, unintuitive, inflexible, obstinate, and circuitous—then interface design matters very much to us.

On the most basic level, design matters because it plays a large role in determining whether we can get our work done. A well-designed tool is one that is easy to interpret and satisfying to use. In fact, many software developers say that the best designs are ones that users never give a second thought about. They describe this quality as *invisibility* and it is the hallmark of effortless user interaction and good design. In contrast, a poorly designed tool is far from invisible, taking far too much time to use and delivering few results for our work in return. Whether an interface design is a good one or a poor one is a complex and involved issue. But one thing is certain for users, issues of design quality begin with a resource's interface.

What Exactly Is an Interface?

An *interface* is the visible piece of a system that a user sees or hears or touches. Users come into contact with an interface when they use a system, often needing to get a task done. Regardless of whether it whirs, spins, speaks, or lights up, an interface exists in one form or another in every system. There are millions of different interfaces that are designed by someone for something. Some interfaces work well for us, while others do not. Don Norman (who is interviewed at the end of this chapter) has written thoroughly and candidly about the interface design of computers, as well as that of commonplace devices. In *The Design of Everyday Things*, Norman even considers the interface of doorknobs.[1] These common devices, depending on the visibility of their design, may reveal how a door works. A well-designed doorknob communicates to its users whether a door should be pushed or pulled. A poorly designed doorknob gives us no clues. When this happens, we must experiment until we figure out how the door

ATMS: The Design of Everyday Banking

Several semesters ago, I taught an introductory seminar on Human-Computer Interaction (HCI) to advanced graduate students in information science. I used an assignment to find out what the untrained eye notices—good and bad—about interface design. During the first class, I gave a brief lecture on interface design. I then sent the students out to evaluate the design of a bank's ATM. For some, this sounded too hard for a first assignment. *What did they possibly know about design?* I gave them some basic guideline questions along with the assignment: Was the ATM usable? How easily did the system support the functions they use often and the ones they use rarely? What aspects of the ATM design were optimal and less than optimal? The following week the students returned with their field observations. Overall, they had mixed reviews about ATMs; some things worked well while others needed more design work. Among their observations:

- A green light around the card entry slot on some ATMs drew their attention to an important starting point.

- Commonly used functions, like withdrawing $40, appeared as first choices on menus, which made navigating a lot more direct and efficient.

- Left-handed users had a tough time with ATMs because the input pad is designed for right-handed users.

- There were hours during the day when the screen became unreadable because of intense glare from the sun shining on the screen.

- Customizing options for operations that many students performed over and over again were non-existent.

It turned out after all that the students did know something about interface design. In fact, many of their observations were quite insightful. Among them, they found that it is reasonable to expect cues for first-time users. They anticipated quick responses from the system. When the screen sat mute after a button was pushed, their interaction with the ATM began to break down. The students' comments revealed an underlying dimension that is true for all user interactions with interfaces: No matter who we are, what system we are using, or what skill level we have mastered, we bring certain expectations to systems about completing some necessary task. When those expectations are not met, then the design begins to fail.

works—sometimes to our own detriment! Norman's point is that well-designed interfaces, no matter what kind of mechanism we are talking about, are based on solid design principles that enhance use. A good design is a reliable and effective intermediary, sending us the right cues so that tasks get done—regardless of how trivial, incidental, or artful the design might seem to be.

Computer interfaces are also important translators of functionality. They work by projecting a simplified, designed version of all of the complex information-processing tasks actually occurring inside the box's circuitry, whether it is withdrawing money from an automated teller machine (ATM), word processing a letter, or viewing a video clip from a Web page. In order to carry out tasks, users type in something through a keyboard or they point and click with a mouse. This aspect of the exchange between a user and an interface is called *interaction*. Once a request has been entered by the user, the computer undergoes several translation stages. Translation occurs at the program level as well as at the circuitry level, funneling a response back to users through the interface. As involved as this electronic dance may seem, processing usually occurs very quickly, owing much to the speed and agility of the microprocessor chip.

Interfaces and Design Language

In the past 20 years, most of us have come to know computer interfaces by what is being communicated to us through a unit's screen. The concept of *design language* describes how interfaces communicate what objects are to users, what they might do, and how they should be used.[2] Just as spoken language is a basis of conversation between people, design language is a basis of communication between designers, users, and interfaces. While spoken language has grammar and words, design language consists of a more narrowly defined set of design elements (icons, for instance), the rules for their combination, and the context in which they exist. An interface design language has three primary parts. First, there are *elements,* (or the icons), color, and functions that appear on the screen. Second, there are *organizing principles,* an interface's grammar, which are the rules for how design elements will be combined to convey meaning. Third, there are *qualifying principles,* or design that takes into account the medium's context and its opportunities and limitations. The Web, for example, has many qualifying principles. On one hand, the Web medium has multimedia opportunities, while on the other, the Web is limited by external factors, such as variability among browsers.

As we saw in the ATM example, what is on the screen (icons, desktops, menus, or cursors) and how these artifacts can be manipulated (through a mouse or a keyboard) make up a system's interface and its design language. The menu that appeared on the ATM is an interface element that is featured in a variety of computer products as a method for navigation. The choice of functions that serve as headings and their layout on a menu are the organizing principles that communicate how the system can be manipulated and controlled by users. In the students' design commentary, they indicated that there are advantages and disadvantages to the ATM environment (such as the way sunlight minimized the readability of the screen during certain times of the day), which make up its qualifying principles. Interface designers and system developers have to choose between each one of these design language components and weigh the trade-offs. The choices that developers make and the impact that they may have on users and how users interact with a system is the basis of the study of Human-Computer Interaction (HCI).

Defining Human-Computer Interaction

Even though HCI is a relatively new field, it shares a long history with the design of artifacts for human use. In particular, HCI is concerned with creating interactive computer systems that are usable. Many of the early concepts in the HCI discipline originated in the late 1970s and 1980s. Ideas came to fruition by way of engineers' efforts at Xerox (and later, Apple and IBM) to build computer-based systems that were more user-centered than engineer-centered. As the field has taken hold, definitions of HCI have become multidisciplinary, technical, and diverse. Nevertheless, there are two general definitions of HCI that are widely agreed upon by practitioners in the field. The first one comes from the lead HCI association, The Curriculum Development Group of the Association for Computing Machinery (ACM) Special Interest Group on Computer-Human Interaction (SIGCHI):

> Human-Computer Interaction is a discipline concerned with the design, evaluation, and implementation of interactive computing systems for human use and with the study of major phenomena surrounding them.[3]

Another definition comes from a leading HCI textbook:

> Human-Computer Interaction (or HCI) is, put simply, the study of people, computer technology, and the ways these influence

each other. We study HCI to determine how we can make this computer technology usable by people.[4]

As both definitions indicate, HCI has two primary dimensions. First, HCI has a dimension that is a practical method that involves user testing during the building and implementing of new systems. The second dimension of HCI is an evaluative study about cognitive and other behavioral factors that come into play when people interact with computers. Each one of these dimensions is interrelated and interdependent. In many cases, formal findings about how people interact with systems generated from the evaluation side of HCI become a basis for decision making about design trade-offs during product development.

Dimensions of HCI

Building Systems

In order to build user-centered systems, developers need to look at users' needs, values, and supportable tasks. This is why the HCI approach involves typical users who participate early on in testing of prototypes and other usability studies with product developers. Even before the actual design process begins, developers following an HCI approach first analyze a product's potential user base and how users are going to utilize the system in their jobs. To get at this information, developers simulate real work situations and prototypes with intended users. HCI researchers ask these five primary questions when building user-centered systems:

- How will design work get done during the development phase?

- How can systems be designed that work better to support users' tasks?

- What design trade-offs exist and what are solutions that support users?

- What can we make that is new?

- Is the system usable?

Evaluating Systems

Besides being a building methodology and technique, HCI is also an evaluative study about the interaction that occurs between people and computers. In the past 20 years, HCI research has been carried out to establish metrics and standards for creating user-centered design. When graphical user interfaces were just being developed, there were many unanswered questions about what rules to apply. HCI researchers played an important role in establishing many standards for predicting users' performance. One example of early empirical HCI research carried out at Xerox's Palo Alto Research Center (PARC) quantified the optimum speed of a mouse in relation to human processing speed. This study was one of the Human Processor Model Studies, groundbreaking work that paired engineering capabilities with human cognitive abilities so that more user-responsive systems could be built.[5]

Disciplinary Origins

Much of HCI research pulls together seemingly disparate fields, such as engineering and cognitive science, to study interaction effects and to recommend design approaches. Yet the core of HCI evaluation is firmly grounded in four major disciplines: computer science, cognitive science, social psychology, and human factors or ergonomics.[6] Each of these primary fields has made a significant contribution in defining the parameters of the HCI subfield.

Computer Science. Computer science delivers the device that creates a need for an interface. Computer science and HCI are deeply intertwined since HCI is actually a component of computer science. Computer science deals with the technological capabilities and the engineering components of computing systems and products, while HCI deals with translating system complexities into interfaces that support users' tasks and capabilities. HCI is chiefly concerned with creating user-centered interfaces that enhance user interactions, while computer science involves automating and processing symbolic information through algorithms. The combined fields have successfully led to automating dimensions of the design process of HCI, including the creation of high-level programming languages, new devices for interaction, and prototyping tools.

Cognitive Science. Cognitive science, a branch of psychology, is the study of how the human behaviors of perception, attention, learning, and memory affect information processing. Cognitive theory plays a seminal role in HCI because it analyzes how people figure out and communicate with computing systems. Many early HCI-based cognitive studies have focused on how people perceive computer systems, especially studying how users go about problem-solving in a computer environment, how their attention is managed, and how users learn and retain operational information over time. Cognitive fundamentals and principles, many of which were developed in the 1980s, have provided much of the early HCI framework.

Social Psychology. Social psychology is the scientific study of how humans behave as groups in social and work settings. HCI work, with a social psychology focus, combines group issues such as organizational structures, power, and authority with HCI issues of how information flows among groups, shared technology, and social contexts. A growing amount of HCI research is rooted in this framework, especially as networked tools like e-mail, groupware, and virtual reality applications have become more commonplace.

Human Factors. Human factors deal with matching the physical characteristics of systems with users' capabilities and capacities. In particular, human factors studies are concerned with training, performance, and behavior and ways to improve the design practicalities of safety and efficiency. Recent human factors research has concentrated on screen readability rates, repetitive stress syndrome and the building of safer systems, and developing emerging interaction styles like voice activation.

HCI as Process

The HCI process deals with creating more usable systems for people and their work settings. Much of the underlying purpose of HCI incorporates good design, both in practice and in understanding. To achieve this goal, HCI is the study of both sides of the interaction experience. By this we mean that HCI addresses what occurs on the human side of interaction as well as what happens on the machine side. Basically, HCI looks at human processing abilities and communication structures that occur between users and their computers. HCI also uncovers methods for mapping computing functions to human capabilities and effectively using input and output techniques so that computers and users have more seamless interactions.

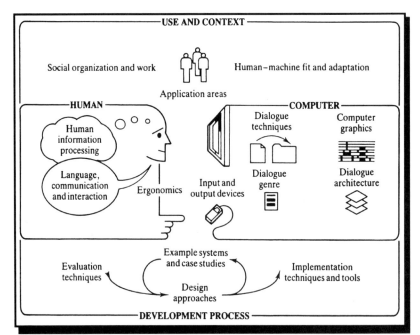

Figure 1.1 is reprinted from *ACM/SIGCHI Curricula for Human-Computer Interaction*, ACM, p. 16, © 1992, used by permission.

Figure 1.1 The Discipline of Human-Computer Interaction

When the SIGCHI chapter of the ACM was in its infancy, the group developed a graphic (shown in Figure 1.1) that illustrates the boundaries of HCI and the interrelationships between the two sides of interaction, the human side and the machine side. The bottom of the graphic shows another dimension of HCI, which deals with how systems are built. HCI puts a special emphasis on creating and applying user-centered design techniques as well as using iterative usability testing methods.

The Relevance of HCI

In recent years, many disciplines have contributed to forming and expanding HCI thought. These disciplines include linguistics, artificial intelligence, anthropology, epistemology, communication, sociology, and graphic design. As a result, HCI has grown as a field and gathered increased support on college campuses, in information technology companies, and among professional computing organizations. The reason for the growing interest in HCI may be long overdue: Fundamentally, HCI is a study that embraces everyday users while making a strong case for developing workable systems for them.

Another way HCI has gained ground is by developing elegant and new solutions that actually transform how people interact with systems. One such development is direct manipulation and the mouse. Direct manipulation is now a commonplace interaction style that allows users to move objects around a computer screen with a mouse, as they would a real object. For users to be able to physically move objects on a screen was an early programming breakthrough for the fledgling HCI field—one that presented point-and-click ease and control of the graphical user interface to a huge number of novice users.

There are also commercial reasons for HCI's acceptance. An interface that outsells the rest—the *killer app* as it is sometimes called—is dependent not only on what an interface can do but also on how it delivers functionality to users. The VisiCalc spreadsheet of the late 1970s was one of the first software killer apps, combining a highly interpretative ledger design (based on what accountants used) with capabilities that processed so quickly that they far exceeded any user's brain power. In other words, HCI is about building better products for users, but often this design goal results in producing more salable ones as well.

HCI clearly has importance beyond the building, designing, and marketing of computer interfaces and systems. At the close of his book, *The Design of Everyday Things*, Norman argues that well-designed interfaces should matter just as much to users as to those who design computer products. He urges readers:

> If you are a user, then join your voice with those who cry for usable products. Write to manufacturers. Boycott unusable designs. Support good designs by purchasing them, even if it means going out of your way, even if it means spending a bit more. And voice your concerns to the stores that carry the products; manufacturers listen to their customers. . . . And enjoy yourself. Walk around the world examining the details of design. Take pride in the little things that help; think kindly of the person who so thoughtfully put them in. Realize that even details matter, that the designers may have had to fight to include something helpful. Give mental prizes to those who practice good design: send flowers. Jeer those who don't: send weeds.[8]

As more and more information resources for computer users appear, design evaluation becomes an essential part of resource selection. The kind of user evaluation that Norman advocates calls for new skills for many would-be evaluators. Design evaluation requires looking up from the price tag to critically assess how systems might actually work for users. Yet the

Table 1.1 The Pick of the Lot: Recommended Readings and Web Sites

Brenda Laurel, ed., *The Art of Human-Computer Interface Design*, Reading, Mass.: Addison-Wesley Publishing Company, 1990.

Donald A. Norman, *The Design of Everyday Things*, New York: Basic Books, 1990.

Jenny Preece, Yvonne Rogers, Helen Sharp, David Benyon, Simon Holland, and Tom Carey, *Human-Computer Interaction*, Harlow, England: Addison-Wesley Publishing Company, 1994.

Terry Winograd with John Bennett, Laura DeYoung, and Bradley Hartfield, eds., *Bringing Design to Software*, Reading, Mass.: Addison-Wesley Publishing Company, 1996.

Special Interest Group on Computer-Human Interaction (SIGCHI) with the Association for Computing Machinery (ACM) Web site. Available http://www.acm.org/sigchi/. This Web site includes links to publications, conferences, other HCI sites, and membership information.

ability to identify products or services with good design features over bad ones has large payoffs in any setting. A well-designed tool means that end users will be able to complete the tasks they need to get done—and usually with less repetitive training and more satisfaction. Most importantly, though, how well designed a resource is often determines whether it will ever get used.

INSIDE . . .

An Interview with Don Norman
About What Design Is

Don Norman, a leading HCI researcher and author of The Invisible Computer: Why Good Products Fail, the Personal Computer Is So Complex and Information Appliances Are the Solution *(1998), is the former head of the Advanced Appliance Design Center at Hewlett-Packard and the former vice president of Apple Computer's Research Laboratories. He is now with the Nielsen Norman Group (http://www.nngroup. com), a consulting firm specializing in user-centered design for software, hardware, and Web interfaces.*

What is design?

It is wrong to think that design has a single dimension. To many people, design means fashions. That's why it is called "the design world." Fashion is indeed an important part of design. Mechanical engineers take design classes too. What they learn is which mechanisms to put together and how to decide. There's also the designing of electrical circuits or designing a program. These are all legitimate kinds of design. Or you can design from the point of the user, where you are making devices understandable, aesthetically pleasing, and able to fulfill the functions that are needed.

If you put it all together, the number of disciplines and kind of knowledge that you have is overwhelming. Design can be very technical, mechanical, artistic, psychological, and commercial. No single person has all of these abilities or knows all of these disciplines. So one of the challenges is to get multiple disciplines to work together harmoniously and to come out with a product.

Is there such a thing as a well-designed tool?

The best-designed tools are hand tools. Traditional hand tools are for woodworking or for gardening. A lot of them are so good because they have taken centuries to be defined. Japanese hand tools are quite exquisite. Their gardening and woodworking tools are very different from American or European tools. In many cases, it is not that their tools are better, it is that their practices are different, so the tool fits that particular practice.

What's the first thing you look at when you're trying to determine whether or not a tool is well designed?

The first thing I ask is whether the tool does the job. The most important thing is whether it has a useful set of functions, whether it does what we expect. And then there's a wide range of variables. Is it aesthetically pleasing? If it is something you hold in your hand, it should feel good. Is there an ease of use?

How should people approach design evaluation?

In the end, there is always a trade-off in design. If people are aware and sensitive to the trade-off, then they can make decisions. It doesn't matter so much if they end up with what I might regard as a wrong decision. What I mind is when users weren't even aware that there was a possible decision that designers had to make. In that sense, everybody is always a designer because everyone is always evaluating the world around them. Nothing is done by accident; even the worst-designed thing has had quite a bit of thought. But in these cases, a lot of this thought is based on the technology or the mechanical difficulties instead of on users and their needs.

Have users become more savvy about what to expect from computer interfaces?

Yes. Users are better educated about information technology. They have certain expectations about the way things will work. The designers have become more savvy too, and they have begun to design things for the more experienced users. The major PC platforms are, for the most part, all graphical user interfaces that are very similar in style. This has aided some things.

But there is a problem. The graphical user interface (GUI) paradigm itself no longer works. Originally it was designed for the Macintosh with a 128K of memory—that's 128,000 words of memory. Today, we could easily have 128 million bytes of memory! It was designed for a floppy disk of 400K, no hard disk, and no networking. Today, we have gigabytes of hard disk and lots of networking. So, when early interfaces were designed, the notion that everything should be visible on the screen—functions and features—made a lot of sense. You would have had twenty files and programs with a small number of commands. Today, you have thousands of files. So the basic fundamental design principle of GUIs itself no longer works.

What does the future hold for computers and interface design?

The PC is the wrong device because it is fundamentally too complex. It is complex for many reasons. In one sense, the PC has to support users all over the world with one single device. There's also the problem for PC makers who have to support their historical legacy. We have tried to make one device that does everything in your life, which requires that it has to do everything for everybody in the world because we sell one device all across the world. It is not possible to know your user if it is the whole world—age, sex, race, economic class, education, vocational level, different needs, and so on. So you get computers with hundreds of thousands of options that the average user would never care much about.

Computers are not fundamentally structured for everyday life. And there will be no magical solutions coming along. We need to get rid of the damn thing and start over again. We need to build devices that do not emphasize the technology but emphasize what people are trying to accomplish. I call these devices *information appliances*, things that fit the way you work. In the early days, you bought one home electric motor for your kitchen from a place like the Sears Roebuck catalog and it came with many attachments. But you don't do that anymore. Today, you have a coffee grinder, you have an egg beater, or a garbage disposal. Each of them is an electric motor and a simple attachment. But we don't think of them in that way. We think of them as something for a task. That's what information appliances should be like. But for information appliances to work right, they will have to talk to each other. It will take around ten years before there are enough information appliances around to make a difference. PCs will still fill a need but probably more with technical people. Only they will need them.

Endnotes

1. Donald A. Norman, *The Design of Everyday Things*, New York: Basic Books, 1990.
2. John Rheinfrank, and Shelley Evenson, "Design Languages," in Terry Winograd with John Bennett, Laura DeYoung, and Bradley Hartfield, eds. *Bringing Design to Software*, Reading, Mass.: Addison-Wesley Publishing Company, 1996, pp. 63–80.
3. T. Hewett, R. Baecker, S. Card, T. Cary, J. Gasen, M. Mantiel, G. Perlman, G. Strong, and W. Verplank, "ACM SIGCHI Curricula for Human-Computer Interaction," *Report of the ACM SIGCHI Curriculum Development Group*, New York: Association for Computing Machinery, 1992.
4. Alan Dix, Jayne Finlay, Gregory Abowd, and Russell Beale, *Human-Computer Interaction*, Englewood Cliffs, N.J.: Prentice Hall, 1993.
5. Stuart Card, Thomas Moran, and Allen Newell, *The Psychology of Human-Computer Interaction*, Hillsdale, N.J.: Lawrence Erlbaum Associates, 1983.
6. My disciplinary breakdown of HCI is based on the classification scheme that appears in: Jenny Preece et al., *Human-Computer Interaction*, Harlow, England: Addison-Wesley Publishing Company, 1994, pp. 37–43.
7. As noted, Figure 1.1 is reprinted from *ACM/SIGCHI Curricula for Human-Computer Interaction*, ACM, New York: Association for Computing Machinery, © 1992, p. 16, used by permission.
8. Norman, op. cit., pp. 216–17.

2 Secret Shame

I n 1990, Mitchell Kapor rocked the computer world. The founder of Lotus Development Corporation and designer of Lotus 1-2-3 delivered the "Software Design Manifesto," telling a crowd of leading computer industry executives his thoughts about computers and their use:

> Scratch the surface and you'll find that people are embarrassed to say they find these devices hard to use. They think the fault is their own. So users learn a bare minimum to get by. They underuse the products we work so hard to make. . . . The lack of usability of software and the poor design of programs are the secret shame of the industry.[1]

A Time for Change

The audience was well aware of the difficulties users face when operating the systems they build. Some cared. Others did not. No matter what Kapor said, they were still making money. Nevertheless, Kapor's address ended up having a transforming effect, especially on what he asked of the group. At the heart of his manifesto, he called for the formal recognition of software design as a profession. This meant that software design needed voluntary industry acknowledgment for the limited number of designers that did exist as well as developing university curricula to train new designers. He told the listeners that creating quality software was not possible without this vital change.

Kapor went on to describe how "the designer leads a guerrilla existence, formally unrecognized and unappreciated."[2] In the companies where they worked, designers were regularly shunned by programmers and engineers during the software development process. Kapor argued that many of those involved in the development process were engineers working to develop software from the inside out, rarely considering users' needs in the building process until it was far too late. Under these conditions, many of the products released ended up being unusable. He urged that software design be integrated into the overall software development process. With his proposed approach to software development, engineers would build systems, programmers would write code, and designers would take on the overall conception of products in ways that supported users' actual needs.

Since his call to arms, the fledgling field of interface design has burgeoned. Many university computer science departments have added courses, acknowledging the value of design in training future computer scientists.[3] Associations promoting software design and its professionalism have cropped up. In particular, the Association for Computing Machinery, the venerable computing society, has added interest groups and initiated journals concerned with the topic of design. Conferences featuring interface design topics have multiplied. But the biggest shot in the arm for the design field may have come through the ever-expanding World Wide Web. As the Web has developed, interest in interface design has grown tremendously. In *Interface Culture*, Steven Johnson, the editor of *Feed*, an online magazine about culture (www.feedmag.com), recently claimed:

Where the Victorian novel shaped our understanding of the new towns wrapped around the steel mill and the cotton gin, and fifties television served as an imaginative guide to the new suburban enclaves created by the automobile, the interface makes the teeming, invisible world of zeros and ones sensible to us. There are few creative acts in modern life more significant than this one, and few with such broad social consequences.[4]

Whether you fully agree with the magnitude of Johnson's statement or not, interface design is experiencing a renaissance. Beyond the traditional domain of creating desktop environments and tools for software packages, a whole new set of designers now find themselves developing full-blown, creative information spaces on the ubiquitous Web. Much of this work is being done with a handful of accessible and inexpensive tools, and is based on hypertext markup language (HTML). Interface design has edged toward center stage, bursting with creativity, as more and more players enter the arena.

The Way Things Used to Be Built

How information technologies, from hardware to software, are developed has changed significantly. In the early days, the 1960s and 1970s, most systems were conceived using the so-called *waterfall model*. This traditional model worked in a tightly wound linear fashion, which in the end was often time-consuming and costly. Over time, the model has been vilified for developing systems with little applicability beyond the small band of people involved with the project and a handful of regular devotees. The waterfall model was made up of phases, each independently carried out, and then tumbled down to set off the next stage. The process started with drawing up a formal plan between developers and clients about what the system would do. Then the building process began. First came an engineering analysis of what the product needed to do and what it could actually accomplish. Next was the system design phase, where the product was built with the builders themselves considered as the "likely users" of the system. In the final steps, documentation was written and the product was tested with a group of outside users.

This former methodology for building systems may sound strange in today's era of rapid prototyping, jump-started by ever-faster computers and seemingly endless venture capital. But the waterfall method worked when military-based funding was plentiful for huge, singular projects. It was when the computer industry commercially evolved and was in need of an innovative, idea-generating model for development that the waterfall model, and its variations, failed miserably. There were several reasons why. First, the waterfall method started out with a formal binding contract, often constraining creativity on both developers' and clients' sides. Second, the linear nature of the method constricted essential communication between the parties developing the system or product. The work necessary to complete each development phase was often done independently—far from the team approach now practiced and ballyhooed in today's management journals. Finally, potential users were brought in for testing the system long after most of the building and refining phases had ended. In other words, users were testing a product that was nearly completed. It was not until the late 1970s that developers began to discover they could build better products if they listened to users sooner.

From Engineering to Designing

Xerox's Palo Alto Research Center (PARC) is at ground zero when it comes to the annals of interface design. This is the heady, elite computer science lab where the first graphical user interface, or GUI, was developed. This, too, is the place where a highly innovative approach to interface design was first instilled. Together, these factors launched a fledgling computer industry that became an economic monolith. The story is almost legendary.

Ideas for a better computing system had long been batted around. Stanford Research Institute's Doug Engelbart had mesmerized many in the computing community as far back as 1968 with his presentation of a revolutionary computing system that featured a working bitmap screen display, live video teleconferencing, networking, and a navigational device called a *mouse.* In one short 90-minute demo, Engelbart transformed the computing paradigm, demonstrating that computers had potential far beyond their number-crunching origins and could function as information spaces where people could work and collaborate.

It was at Xerox's PARC, though, where these fluid, industry-wide ideas first coalesced. On the research side of the lab, Alan Kay had built the Alto, regarded by many as the first personal computer with a GUI interface. The Development Division at Xerox seized the Alto project, transforming it into a commercial opportunity. In 1978, Xerox decided to combine the Alto with other significant Xerox work into a salable product—the Star 8010.[5]

The Star took three long years to build, a design schedule that is unheard of in today's hardware and software development companies. But the wait was worth it. The Star was impressive, showcasing Xerox's finest work all in one system. The Xerox Star was decidedly a new device, unlike anything that came before. Most widely acknowledged was the Star's break from the cumbersome mainframe and its arcane command language, providing users with a graphical user interface that included overlapping windows, icons, pull-down menus, and a mouse, giving users a sense of more control. The system also ran on one of the world's first networks, an Ethernet, and premiered another whole new product, the laser printer.

Ironically, though, the Star was a dismal commercial failure. One cause was the system's high cost. In today's dollars, the price tag would roughly be about $15,000 for the system, plus another $15,000 for the printer. Another reason was the Star's proprietary nature, keeping other companies from making accessory products, like software. In fact, it took another entrepreneur, Apple co-founder Steven Jobs, to fully appreciate the seductiveness of a graphical interface. In the early 1980s, farther down the road from Xerox's PARC, Jobs went about stripping away the functionalities of the Star to create his own products—first, the Lisa and later the Macintosh, a "computer for the rest of us." In Washington state, an increasingly anxious competitor, Bill Gates, grabbed onto the systematic advantages of the Star's overlapping windows environment, launching the most profitable software package ever, Microsoft Word.

Even though the Star fell short in the marketplace, the methodology used for building the system caused a great stir within the computer industry, changing it forever. The Star was not just programmed and assembled. The system was carefully and meticulously designed with about as much attention as a first-time mother gives a newborn. Before development even began, a group was pulled together to specifically study and write a methodology for creating something entirely new—a *user* interface. The group of engineers came up with a methodology that was directly contrary to the earlier waterfall method.

Instead of following a path that ended with a completed system and some testing of users, the Star project began with a task analysis of how and why users would use a system. The developers looked at a wide range of potential users who were office workers and laid out the task scenarios of writing memos and reports that the employees would try to complete with the system. The team then wrote 400 pages of functional specification before they ever wrote a line of programming code and over 600 painstaking hours of videotape were filmed of actual users interacting with and using every single feature and function.[6] The development team continually prototyped versions of the Star on real users, altering the system on almost every turn with the help of engineers, designers, and psychologists. Through the development and testing of this uniquely visual interface, the Star group ushered in canonical design principles for graphical interfaces and the foundations of *user-centered design*.

The User-Centered Design Methodology

User-centered is the mantra of the Human-Computer Interaction (HCI) approach to interface design. When user-centered design principles are applied, end users are involved early on and throughout the development process. The user-centered design process is highly iterative to insure that the design fits users' expectations about functionality and operations. Before they get very far, project developers need to decide who their end users are and how the interface may be used. Once they have prototyped a product, developers conduct user testing that informs them about the effectiveness of their design choices. The user-centered approach is a methodology that includes parallel testing and measurement techniques that are based on design guidelines. An approach to the user-centered process, developed at IBM research for developing products, is detailed in Figure 2.1 (see page 28).[7]

As Figure 2.1 suggests, a user-centered approach is lengthy and can be wrought with ferreting out design dilemmas, weighing trade-offs, and redesigning the product. To resolve the complexities that naturally arise during the development process, user-centered design integrates knowledge from beyond the software engineering field. Cognitive science—or how people perceive and process information—often becomes an essential element early in the development of user systems. Working with other specialists, usually psychologists, developers measure the cognitive effects of a design. Depending on the product, they may analyze physiological constraints that exist for users, too. Typical questions asked might be: Does a screen layout help users make quick decisions or does it overwhelm and distract? What do we know about the interaction process with similar tools that already exist?

In large companies, such as Sun and Microsoft, usability labs often play a central role in improving products during development. Usability engineers apply a number of tests, including protoyping, card sorting, and videotaping,

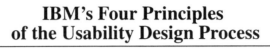

IBM's Four Principles
of the Usability Design Process

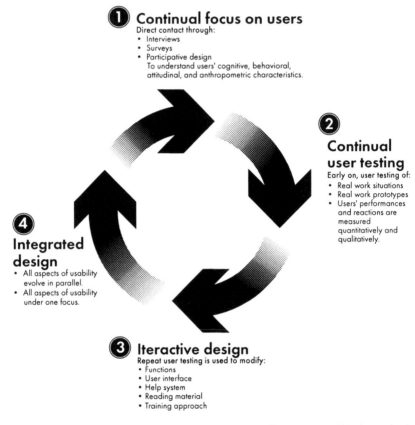

① Continual focus on users
Direct contact through:
* Interviews
* Surveys
* Participative design
To understand users' cognitive, behavioral, attitudinal, and anthropometric characteristics.

② Continual user testing
Early on, user testing of:
* Real work situations
* Real work prototypes
* Users' performances and reactions are measured quantitatively and qualitatively.

④ Integrated design
* All aspects of usability evolve in parallel.
* All aspects of usability under one focus.

③ Iteractive design
Repeat user testing is used to modify:
* Functions
* User interface
* Help system
* Reading material
* Training approach

Source: Graphical depiction of the ideas presented in John Gould, "How to Design Usable Systems," in Ronald Baecker, Jonathan Grudin, William S. Buxton, and Saul Greenberg, eds. *Readings in Human-Computer Interaction: Toward the Year 2000*, San Francisco: Morgan Kaufman Publishers, Inc., 2nd ed., 1995, p. 95.

Figure 2.1   Considerable Factors in the HCI Approach to Interface Design

to study what happens to real users when they try to use systems and software to carry out real-life tasks. (See the interview at the end of this chapter with Sun Microsystems' former usability engineer, Jakob Nielsen.) Behavioral testing methods are developed and applied by usability engineers to technically study otherwise subjective design qualities, such as user friendliness, learnability, and intuitiveness. The results give developers a guideline for what works and what needs improvement while products are

---

Table 2.1 *IBM's Behavioral Test and Specifications for Getting a PC Up and Running*

Test participants, a random sample from customers who are willing to participate in this experiment, must be able to unpack this prototype home computer and connect the display, printer, mouse, keyboard, and special effects card. They must initiate the system and then set the date and time on the computer. This work must be completed by at least 17 of the 20 participants in 60 minutes, using only the instructions contained in the manuals in the box.

---

being developed. Table 2.1 shows an example of a task developed at IBM Research that is used to evaluate product user friendliness for new PC buyers.

As the example in Table 2.1 shows, usability researchers are particularly interested in measuring ease of learning and task accomplishment as well as establishing standards for expected performance. Findings from tests like this one are reported to developers working on systems so that products being developed, as well as future products, can be improved. There are often surprises in findings about how users perceive and actually use products, which then change the course of product development, as the sidebar about Microsoft shows (see page 30).

In Search of User-Centered Design

Despite dedication to user-centered design approaches, many companies have trouble living up to the elusive endeavor for a variety of reasons. Alan Cooper, the developer of Visual Basic, has argued that the trouble with designing user-centered commercial software paradoxically remains a conflicting mix of part user-centered design and part programming. On one hand, developers may well be concerned with how a software product will communicate and work for a user, which is a user-centered approach. Yet on the other hand, the same developer is integrally involved in the actual construction of the product, which is a code-writing or

Microsoft: Simplify, Simplify

Problems with making usable products? It is hard to believe that the mega-software giant, Microsoft, would worry about such things. The company's ubiquitous suite of software, Microsoft Office 95, which includes such indispensable programs as Word, Excel, and PowerPoint, has carved out 90 percent of the market share and counts 22 million users worldwide.[8] In a good week, Microsoft Office 95 outsells any other competitor by a 15 to 1 margin.[9]

Nevertheless, when it came to designing Microsoft 97, the Microsoft crew put in 25,000 hours of research in an effort to improve their latest offering of the software suite product.[10] The company collected large amounts of user data from a variety of available sources, including usage studies, product support calls (of which they receive 20,000 calls a day), usability testing, user input, and other specialized testing procedures.[11] Their collective findings delivered some surprising results to product developers, which changed the course of the product's development.

All along, Microsoft's design strategy for the Office product was to offer an abundance of features to wanting users. At first, the Office suite package was designed as a series of stand-alone applications that were bundled together for convenience.[12] But it soon became clear that users wanted integrated applications that worked well together. In fact, 80 percent of Microsoft 95 users reported using more than one of the Microsoft suite applications when creating a document.[13] The development group also discovered that users, over and over again, clamored for easier, more intuitive software from the company. Worse yet, the group also found that most users, barring their level of expertise, were totally unaware of the full functionality of Microsoft's products. Microsoft's programs had become so laden with features, that users could not figure out whether the programs could do the tasks they needed to get done.

A primary design goal for the Office 97 release was to make users, who have become a ubiquitous mix of beginners and intermediate level users, more self-reliant and to get more out of each product. One direct result was the introduction of a motley crew of nine agent-based, online characters. The characters, dubbed Office Assistants, were designed as a new approach to user assistance (a user sore spot with Microsoft products for some time). The characters were touted by Microsoft as online advisors that encouraged independent learning for users seeking help and that helped users accomplish tasks more efficiently. But for Microsoft, achievement of the goal may have fallen short. A majority of product reviews dismissed the characters as annoying and mettlesome pests that got in the way of the tasks at hand.[14]

programming function. Often these two jobs have goals that are at odds, requiring decidedly different sensibilities. Under these conditions, Cooper writes:

> Most software is built like crazy Mrs. Winchester's house, who thought that she'd die if she ever stopped building. Rooms and stairs and cupboards and walls are added in manic confusion as the need and opportunity presents itself during construction. Programmers, deep in their thoughts of algorithms and coding arcana, design user interfaces the way miners design the landscape with their cavernous pits and enormous tailing piles. The software design process alternates between the accidental and the nonexistent.[15]

Considerable Factors
in the HCI Approach to Interface Design

1. Organizational factors:
Training, job design, politics, roles, work organization

10. Productivity factors:
Increase output, increase quality, decrease costs,
decrease errors, decrease labor requirements,
decrease production time, increase creative and
innovative ideas leading to new products

2. Environmental factors:
Noise, heating, lighting, ventilation

9. System functionality:
Hardware, software, application

HCI approach

3. Health and safety factors:
Stress, headaches,
musculoskeletal disorders

8. Constraints:
Costs, timescales, budgets,
staff, equipment, building
structure

4. Cognitive aspects of the user:
Motivation, enjoyment, satisfaction,
personality, experience level

7. Task factors:
Easy, complex, novel, task allocation,
repetitive, monitoring, skills, components

5. Comfort factors:
Setting, equipment layout

6. User interface:
Input devices, output displays, dialogue structures, use of color,
icons, commands, graphics, natural language, 3-D,
user support materials, multimedia

Source: Graphical depiction of the ideas presented by Jenny Preece et al., *Human-Computer Interaction*, Harlow, England: Addison-Wesley Publishing Company, 1994, p. 31.

Figure 2.2   Considerable Factors in the HCI Approach to Interface Design

Another reason that the HCI design approach remains difficult to carry out is that the many HCI factors related to good design may, in fact, contradict one another. Figure 2.2 shows all of the factors that must be considered when designing with an HCI approach.[16]

As Figure 2.2 implies, the factors are many, and contradictions can arise depending on the product, the team members, the end users, or the company where the product is being developed. Making careful trade-offs between these numerous factors, while supporting design principles and approaches, remains a challenge of the HCI field.

But, an HCI approach to design can also be squelched beyond the design arena. User-centered design can easily be discouraged in large organizations by the sheer number of people allocated to building and designing products. Compounding this problem, different teams often develop and design projects using software and systems that are not compatible with other projects. In other words, the small, meticulous Star-like team is more of an ideal these days than a given. Also there are the complications of corporate empires, where profitability pressures, disfunctional corporate cultures, and the retention of a competitive edge can all impede a thoughtful user-centered, design methodology.

Today, most designers would advocate a development methodology that puts the user at center stage. Nonetheless, as we have seen, the practice of actually building and designing products is often in direct conflict with

---

Table 2.2 The Pick of the Lot: Recommended Readings and Web Sites

Jeff Johnson, Terry Roberts, William Verplank, David C. Smith, Charles Irby, and Kevin Mackey. "Xerox Star: A Retrospective," *IEEE Computer*, vol. 22, no. 9, Sept. 1989, pp. 11–9.

Steven Johnson. *Interface Culture: How New Technology Transforms the Way we Create and Communicate*. San Francisco: Harper Edge, 1997.

Jakob Nielsen. *Usability Engineering*. Boston: Academic Press, 1993.

Jakob Nielsen. "Usability Testing of WWW Designs." Sun Microsystems Web site. Available http://www.sun.com/sun-on-net/uidesign, then search by title to get directly to reading.

Alan Cooper. *About Face: The Essentials of User Interface Design*. Foster City, Calif.: IDG Books Worldwide, Inc., 1995.

user-centered principles that are valued and pursued. The relevance of all of this to consumers is a marketplace full of well-intentioned products, each promising user satisfaction but falling very short of the ideal. More than ever, consumers need to know how to distinguish good design from bad.

INSIDE . . .

An Interview with Jakob Nielsen About Usability Testing

Jakob Nielsen, a leading usability engineer and author of Designing Web Sites with Authority: Secrets of an Information Architect *(1998), is the former Distinguished Engineer at Solaris software for Sun Microsystems. He is now with the Nielsen Norman Group (http://www. nngroup.com), a consulting firm specializing in user-centered design for software, hardware, and Web interfaces.*

What is usability testing and why is it necessary?

Usability provides exposure to real users and how they think about your product and its design. It's a way of breaking out of a hole in the company shell because otherwise during development you, as a person on the project, are very internally focused. Usability allows you to get external information about how other people see your design.

Who is the average user anyway?

The term is really "representative user." It depends completely on the project who ends up being our representative users. If it is an intranet project for your company, then the users are the other employees. If you are designing a product for sale, then those customers are the users. Hopefully, the company will have some understanding of who their customers are. You may have a list of registered users, dealers that know customers, or you may employ a focus group company to contact users based on what kinds of things they do.

Does testing take a long time? What's involved?

It does not take a long time at all. In fact, you want a quick feedback loop with people involved in the project so that the turnaround time between testing, implementing the changes, and meeting deadlines is not slowed down.

The most simple example of actual testing is when you already have a design in place. For example, take an old Web site that you are trying to redesign. You get people in and have them use it. Three to five representative users is the quantity I usually recommend. With about an hour of testing, you have already learned a whole lot about this design. When you test, you want to give users three or four specific tasks. If you were testing an airline site, the task might be to look up the cheapest fare to London. But you never say to the user, "Here's a Web site, just play with it." You want to see people use a system to accomplish some typical tasks that people are going to want to do with the product anyhow.

What do you mean when you say that you begin by testing the old version first?

That is the best prototype of your next version of the site. The old site is already implemented, fully working, probably has thousands of pages on it, and also has a lot of depth and detail. So you want to know which things people have difficulty with when they use the site and also with which things they do not have difficulties. You're after things that they like and that support their tasks very well. Then in the redesign, you use the good aspects of the old design and rework the bad aspects. This is only a day's worth of work. You end up knowing a lot about your old design, while giving direction to the new design, too.

What is difficult about your job as a usability tester?

The trouble is that people on the project do not always accept the truth about the findings. User testing is guaranteed to present information about what is good or bad about design, what people want, and what people do. The methods have been proven over twenty years. What is difficult is when you tell other people on the project this is what we have found and they may or may not believe it. Our recommended approach is to have developers come in and sit in on the test, observing the testing of users. This way, as observers, they can get firsthand exposure to the data. They can even watch when a user is not able to accomplish a certain task. When you see this happen firsthand, it can be a powerful experience.

What will the Web do to the concept of user-centered design?

User-centered design is gaining in importance. It used to be that design was only an issue for software designers. But now, every Web site is a user interface or an interactive piece of computer software. Every company that has a Web page needs to have user-centered design as part of its Web development practices. Most Web sites are utter failures because companies don't consider users. Instead, their sites are internally focused. So for people inside the company, the design seems logical but has nothing to do with what a customer wants to do or how they think about the problem.

The Web exposes your company to the customer in a software form. The site becomes your sales force, marketing material, service support, and storefront. If your design is not easy to use, nobody is going to do business with you. Customers will soon have hundreds of millions of other Web sites to which, at a click of a mouse, they can go. The burden of going elsewhere is very low on the Web, which means that the requirement for utter simplicity and ease of use in design will go up dramatically.

Where will usability testing be in ten years?

Usability studies will be widely used for many more products and projects. Usability will be used in schools. Kids will be taught how to do basic usability tests in the fourth or fifth grade. They will develop their own Web sites rather than write assignments on paper, and then they will see how usable it is, maybe by having the class come over from the next room to do the testing. Usability is a basic business skill for the next century. The methods are so basic and won't change even as the technology changes. You get representative people, have them do representative tasks, and see what's easy and what's difficult. Anyone can do usability testing on some level, and should. In the near future, there will be more testing with people in other countries to see how your product is used.

Endnotes

1. Mitchell Kapor, "A Software Design Manifesto," (1990) reprinted in Terry Winograd, with John Bennett, Laura DeYoung, and Bradley Hartfield, eds. *Bringing Design to Software*. Reading, Mass.: Addison-Wesley Publishing Company, 1996, p. 3. Also, see Terry Winograd et al.'s discussion of the influence of Kapor's speech on the development of HCI in *Bringing Design to Software*, op. cit., pp. xiii–xxv.
2. Kapor, op. cit., p. 5.
3. Carnegie-Mellon University, for instance, created a Human-Computer Interaction Department in 1997 that has curriculum focused on training system designers.
4. Steven Johnson, *Interface Culture: How New Technology Transforms the Way We Create and Communicate*, San Francisco: Harper Edge, 1997, p. 17.
5. For a discussion of the Star project see David Liddle, "Design of the Conceptual Model," in Winograd, op. cit., pp. 17–36.
6. Liddle, op. cit., p. 22.
7. Figure 2.1 is a graphical representation of the ideas presented by John D. Gould in "How to Design Usable Systems," In Ronald Baecker, Jonathan Grudin, William S. Buxton, and Saul Greenberg, eds. *Readings in Human-Computer Interaction: Toward the Year 2000*, San Francisco: Morgan Kaufman Publishers, Inc., 2nd ed., 1995, p. 95.
8. "Reviewer's Guide," *Microsoft Office 97*, Redmond Wash.: Microsoft Corporation, Jan. 1997, p. 1.
9. Ibid.

10. "Microsoft 97," *Microsoft Office User Research Report*, Redmond, Wash.: Microsoft Corporation, 1997, p. 1.

11. Microsoft, op. cit., p. 2.

12. Microsoft, op. cit., p. 6.

13. Ibid.

14. For product reviews see Andrew Leonard, "Tough Room for the 'Toons,'" *Salon Magazine*, May 21, 1997. Available http://www.salonmagazine.com/may97/21st/articleb970501.html. 18 Feb. 1999, and Richard Scoville, "Office Assistant: Dog or Genius?" *PC World*, February 1997, http://www.pcworld.com/software/software_suites/articles/feb97/1502p106ff.html. 21 Feb. 1999.

15. Alan Cooper, *About Face: The Essentials of User Interface Design*, Foster City, Calif.: IDG Books Worldwide, Inc., 1995, p. 22.

16. Figure 2.2 is a graphical depiction of the ideas presented by Jenny Preece, Yvonne Rogers, Helen Sharp, David Benyon, Simon Holland, and Tom Carey in *Human-Computer Interaction*, Harlow, England: Addison-Wesley Publishing Company, 1994, p. 31.

Note: Date following Web citations indicates date of access.

3 Deconstructing Evaluation

F
ifteen years ago, there was not much to say about evaluating the design of information resources for computers. Multimedia was in its infancy and there were few products on the market to compare. The small band of users who had access to computer-based information resources was largely made up of professional researchers, librarians, students, and a handful of academics. Their common goal was to unearth content, wherever the information might be buried and under whatever conditions it might take. These pioneer searchers did not give much thought to interface design—how an interface looked and what it was like to use. What counted was access to content.

Back then, many users marveled at how vast amounts of information could be delivered through the circuitry of an electronic box. It was darned seductive. For information professionals, buying-in was awfully easy, too. Evaluation consisted of seeing a product's potential use, making a case for it, and then signing a purchase order, as long as the funding was in place.

In the halcyon days of Grolier's first CD encyclopedia in the mid-1980s and through the early 1990s, commercial competition within the multimedia industry was tame, making the evaluation process for users all the more simple and straightforward. The commercial world of computer-based information products and services was a place where few toes got stepped on and elbow nudges were at a minimum. Even so, some rivalries existed. The tensions between the commercial online providers like Nexis and Dialog and which rights to which content they held were well known. But for the most part, the business of selling information resources to computer users was small and safe. Products and services rarely overlapped in the kind of information they offered. If a company was well placed and provided hard-to-find information that had value, they were a shoo-in for survival. The business model for the time was one based on exclusivity. A company like Reuters, for instance, made a good profit by selling a constant feed of stock quotes to subscribers. In fact, many in the finance industry considered the up-to-date information no lessthan essential.

Keystrokes of Change

Then came the Web. No other communication medium—barring Johannes Gutenberg's printing press—has transformed the public's expectations about information access as much as the World Wide Web has. Now stock quote feeds, a minute or so delayed, are available for free on most financial Web sites. The continually expanding abundance of information— at a rate that doubles in volume every 100 days—delivered at next-to-nothing costs, wherever and whenever users dial up, has set in motion changes that will long be unwinding.[1] But one outcome of the Web is already clear. The old guard experts, who had long relied on their computers as information delivery devices, now have been joined by a huge population of everyday end users who are curious, able, demanding, and, at times, overwhelmed yet seemingly insatiable.

More and more, an information-hungry ilk of end users is finding information available to them in a variety of formats, as the sidebar about Amazon.com shows. Even when it comes to the most incidental of products, like street maps, the phenomenon still holds. For a long time, street maps

Amazon.com: One for the Books

The story goes that Jeff Bezos, the 30-something founder of Amazon.com, first considered creating a Web retail site for music.[2] But he feared that the music industry, which is controlled by a few labels, might put him out of business if the competition became too stiff. Books were a better bet. There were thousands of book publishers, scrambling to promote their products and willing to offer a good break on pricing. The young New York investment banker's hunches about the Web were a boon.

Within a year of its launch in July 1995, Amazon.com had quickly earned household name status. Sales surged, increasing 10-fold from $15.8 million for 1996 to $147.8 million for 1997.[3] Loyalty abounded. Of the 1.5 million customer accounts the business touted by the end of 1997, 58 percent were repeat customers.[4] And in mid-1998, when nothing seemed insurmountable, Amazon.com started retailing music on its site, too.

Much of Amazon.com's initial success was derived from its ability to capitalize on the growing acceptance of Web-based transactions. But the brilliance of Amazon.com is its use of one medium, the Web, to create a community marketplace for selling another medium, the printed book. In a world where information is just a keyboard touch away, book sales are booming. And users of the Amazon site can do more than just order books. They can read online reviews, post their own review, search for books, and even receive book recommendations that are based on their reading tastes and previous choices. Amazon.com is an example of a virtual community that caters to the influx of computer users looking for convenience, ease of use, and value-added information.

were a print product, cheap and handy for stuffing in an automobile glove compartment. But now with multimedia, street maps have turned up in CD and Web site versions too. In fact, one of the most valued sites on Yahoo!, the

popular Internet search directory, is "Yahoo! Maps," a handy site that creates
a map on the fly when a user inputs a couple of addresses. As expansion of
the map business shows, the more perceived usefulness information has, the
more users want the content. Better yet, users have also come to expect
value-added content available to them in a variety of formats. On a regular
basis, Web-savvy searchers peruse the Web expecting to find what they
need—a newspaper article, a currency conversion program, a book review,
or course listings at the local junior college—in a format that is easier to
locate and use than their off-line, original print counterparts.

The influx of information products and services recently led a reporter
for *The Economist* to write that "information, once closely hoarded in many
industries, is becoming a commodity."[5] But information is actually more
than a commodity; it is the basis of a profit model with business acumen.
Many of the information-intensive companies, especially newspapers and
reference publishers that own full rights to their content, have recycled their
existing content for some time, making it available on CDs, Web sites, and
commercial databases such as Nexis. When the creation of multimedia spin-
off products first started gaining speed on the Web several years ago, some
critics warned that new media products, in general, would cannibalize the
business's core product. So far, diversification has both helped to line
corporate coffers and capture different audience segments that were once
out of reach. Newspapers are a prime example. With their Web sites, many
papers have expanded their advertising base and revenues and have captured
a small percentage of younger audiences' readership, a segment that has long
avoided their print products.

But changes brought on by new media (especially the Web) have other
effects on users that cannot be entirely ignored. For many, the proliferation
of information has created an overwhelming and unwieldy information
glut.[6] All of these changes—the increased usage of computers for accessing
value-added information resources, the drastic growth in the end-user base,

and the creation of more and more multimedia products—have created more and more access (as Reva Basch notes in her interview at the end of this chapter). What is actually occurring now is an *access explosion* instead of an *information explosion*. The access explosion is characterized by boundless information products and services, many of which are morphed versions of their primary sources. It is not so much that original content, per se, is increasing in voluminous amounts. It is more that newly developed depositories, such as the Web, are making new content—and a lot of existing content—available in a centralized source for the first time.

Evaluation Revisited

The transformation brought on by new media has put a definite spin on resource evaluation. In short, there are more products to choose from and a more diverse user base, which tends to be overwhelmed by the information choices available to them. This does not mean, however, that the age-old methods for choosing resources should be cast aside. There will always be value in methods that assess whether the resource is packed full of sought-after facts and figures and whether a resource fits decidedly well into a wanting collection. A cost-benefit analysis is essential, too. Resources should be judged on whether they are a good value compared to where else the same information can be had. Candor will always have a role in selection, starting at a gut level and just deciding whether a product is simply easy, fun, or quick to use. There is no doubt that all of these types of questions, when asked in unison, will help contribute to a sound decision.

But these approaches to evaluation overlook an increasingly important dimension of the selection process. As more and more information products and services are becoming available, choosing among resources has become more complex and involved. The evaluation process needs to be deconstructed. An old question of evaluation used to be: "What is the name of the provider that carries the stock feed?" This question is couched in the old business model of online delivery that assumes near-exclusive ownership of data. Less than ten years ago, there was typically only one provider that handled a source's full-text content. The *New York Times* is an infamous example. For a decade, Nexis held the *Times* to an iron-clad agreement that gave the commercial online provider sole proprietary rights to disseminating the newspaper's full-text content online. Few exclusive agreements, such as these, exist anymore. Instead, many content providers—especially newspapers, journals, magazines—have filled up their dance cards with a variety of information purveyors that have issued their content in different packages and provided royalty payments in return. Consequently, evaluation questions about resources have changed. The primary evaluation question has now become: "Out of all the stock feeds available out there (or out of all the places I can get the *Times*), which is the easiest resource to use?" Evaluation increasingly addresses the usability of resources and interface design.

For many evaluators, questions about use and interaction are uncharted waters. Without an understanding of interface design basics, there is a concern among some evaluators that analyzing the design dimension may be a waste of time. Asking a group of users what they think of a particular resource could reap subjective, individualistic, and context-sensitive responses that are of little value when it comes down to choosing resources. Even figuring out where to start when plotting a worthwhile course for evaluating design can be a challenge. But design evaluation can easily be demystified; evaluators should start the process with an area they typically know well—users and their needs.

Defining the User Base

Aristotle knew the importance of users when he wrote that "audience is everything." Despite the technological leaps forward since the philosopher's time, the wise adage still applies, especially when it comes to both carrying out and evaluating interface design. Quite basically, a knowledge of design principles is not enough; understanding users matters, too. For designers there are strengths to using design principles in the development of products but there are also detriments to relying solely on these guidelines. In fact, one interface design article gives this warning:

> Simply rehearsing these principles as though they define an ideal interface archetype, without understanding the practical concerns of the users for whom they are implemented, serves only to belabor the obvious. Of course, an interface must put the user in control, address the user's skill level, operate consistently, be organized logically, and employ sound graphic design. Still, a variety of pressing practical considerations—especially a user base comprising widely disparate users' skill levels— quickly complicates the application of seemingly straightforward design rules.[7]

As the quote suggests, a thorough understanding of the user base is important when designing as well as evaluating resources for selection. We argue here that whoever is conducting an evaluation must have a clear understanding of the potential users, their skill levels, their work setting, and the tasks they need to get done. Evaluators should look carefully at the range of functions offered by an interface to determine what users can do with the tool, whom the tool is intended for, and which tasks are supported and how well. The more thorough the audience assessment, the better the match between users and the resource is likely to be.

There are a few basic things to consider about users during a design evaluation. Table 3.1 (see page 46) displays ten questions that need to be asked about users during the first stages of the evaluation process. As the table shows, whether an interface qualifies as being usable or not may heavily

Table 3.1 Ten Questions to Ask When Defining a Resource's User Base

To ask about the resource:	To ask about the users and the setting:
• What main tasks does the resource support?	• What tasks are users counting on getting done with the resource?
• What level of users is the resource aimed at?	• What skill levels best describe the users (novice, intermediary, expert)?
• Is the resource a tool for users with a certain expertise (e.g., professional graphic artists) or is it a general tool?	• Is there a match between the resource's purpose and the users' needs from a resource?
	• What training will be provided, in addition to the resource's training features or guides?
	• Will the resource be an end-user tool or will hands-on assistance be provided?
	• Does the resource run on platforms that users are familiar with?
	• What processing limitations about the user base can you identify?

depend on a user group's skill level and breadth of experience with other interfaces. When conducting a design evaluation of any interface, questions about the proficiency of the intended user base need to be addressed. Are the users less experienced with computer-based systems? Or are they well versed in the operationality of systems? Or are they a mix of the two? If a resource is introduced to a savvy set of users instead of beginners, the interface may turn out to be more easily learned and retained. This often happens because experienced users can draw knowledge from experiences about how other systems work and apply it to the new situation. Experienced users are usually more willing to experiment, within the confines of what they know first-hand, than beginners. With beginners, the same resource may be regarded as far less usable because these users have a lack of context. If a resource is going to be an end-user resource with little or no hands-on training nearby, the interface needs to support how users figure out and interact with a system. Poorly designed online help systems or feedback functions only confound beginners and casual users trying to learn even more.

Evaluators also need to know about users and the kinds of tasks they seek to support. This is a multifaceted question. There are the tasks themselves, but there is more to consider. Assessing users and tasks involves knowing the kinds of tasks users need to accomplish and the kinds of tasks users are involved with beyond the resource. If users are graphic artists, for instance, then they will need resources with more precision and production options. In this case, output options can also become a critical variable. The expertise of the user base needs to be acknowledged because it will characterize many users' expectations about a system.

Another crucial aspect to think about when defining the intended user base of a product is processing limitations that might exist. Even though disabilities may be difficult to ferret out, there are a couple of givens about any user base. In particular, a certain number of people in any user base will be color-blind. About 8 percent of males and .05 percent of females have difficulty differentiating among colors, especially those on a screen.[8] Interfaces that use color coding for grouping items together can be a problem. Combining several shades of blue on one screen may also be problematic, especially among middle-aged and older users, who typically have a lessened ability to distinguish between shades of blue. Color, too, has cultural connotations that may affect its interpretation, depending on the vastness and diversity of a user base. Finally, the size of fonts and icons, especially as it affects readability, is an important issue. Since it is impossible to know how every user will perceive the graphical elements of an interface, a good rule of thumb when choosing resources is to look at whether aesthetic features can be customized to fit users' individual preferences and needs.

The Basics: Task Support, Usability, and Aesthetics

Once a more thorough understanding of an intended user base is gained, evaluating the design of the interface itself can begin. So far in this book, we have argued that Human-Computer Interaction (HCI) has tremendous applicability for assessing information resources. Mainly, HCI research has shown what happens to users, behaviorally and physically, when they interact with all types of interfaces. Typically, HCI findings are generated and applied to make better products and services. But HCI has relevance as an evaluation tool, too. By applying HCI concepts, better choices about products and services can be made from a user perspective. In particular, when HCI principles and standards are applied to analyze resources during the evaluation process, the likelihood of user satisfaction is more systematically revealed. In this section, basic HCI concepts provide a framework for beginning the design evaluation process of graphical user interfaces (GUIs). Three seminal HCI basics—*task support, usability,* and *aesthetics*—serve as conceptual anchors in our design evaluation template. Each of these HCI concepts and its associated principles fundamentally describe a resource's potential for usefulness.

Task Support

Assessing task support is a central part of evaluating computer-based information resources. To understand task support is to appreciate the implicit contract that exists between a developer, an interface, and a user if a user-centered approach is carried out during product development. A user-centered interface, with the contract in place, delivers the task support that users expect. This is different from support for *any* tasks users may think up. An interface must effectively support the main task users have come to expect from how the resource is marketed, presented, and described. If an interface fails to accurately communicate its purpose to users, whether their skill level is at beginning or expert levels, then it is of very little value to anyone. This is why it becomes important to define user base in terms of the tasks users need and expect to get done. Take, for instance, a multimedia encyclopedia CD-ROM. With this resource, users should expect certain things. For starters, they most undoubtedly expect the CD will have a lot of useful information which is easy to locate. As a result, layout and searching functions become important design features that users expect to work well.

Overall, there are fundamental design benchmarks for task support and information resources. The interface's primary functions, which to a large extent should match what users want to do, should be easy to locate, to comprehend, and to execute. A well-designed interface, for instance, will have headings that are easily differentiated from one another and that clearly list primary functions (e.g., searching). In other words, users should know immediately what the interface's main purpose is and what they can do with the resource. A general rule of thumb in user-centered design is to design so that users' information processing abilities are enhanced. An often-cited finding long applied in traditional interface screen layout is the "magical number seven."[10] The concept is based on research that shows that most people are unable to recall more than seven different numbers or words because of the limited span of their short-term memory. The finding affects menu design, which is a crucial aspect of task support, because it communicates what kind of work is supported. Menus with more than seven different choices are going to be difficult for the majority of users to remember. In general, to evaluate whether an interface communicates

Task Support: The Daily Planet Web Page

Version A

Version B

Figure 3.1   Task Support—Two Views of The Daily Planet *Web Page*

Figure 3.1 shows an example of two versions of design for an opening screen of *The Daily Planet*, a hypothetical newspaper home page on the Web. Which one of these designs offers better task support?

The answer is Version A. Version A puts users' task needs first. Indisputably, one of the typical reasons that users turn to newspaper sites is to find out the day's news. Accordingly, Version A supports this main task by placing the "News" button prominently in the left-hand corner on a black, contrasted background so that users see it first and can begin their work right away. Ben Shneiderman, a leading HCI researcher, writes that "the primary goal for menu designers is to create a sensible, comprehensible, memorable, and convenient semantic organization relevant to the users' tasks."[11] Even though Version A is using a navigation bar instead of a menu, the design still adheres to Shneiderman's design principles because it supports users' tasks with a straightforward design.

The design of Version A further communicates functionality to users through its raised task buttons. In HCI, a raised button is said to have an *affordance* because the graphic element implies action. In other words, the design of the button sends a cognitive clue, through its shading, to users that the object is operational—it can be pressed or clicked on. Affordances can make a subtle but important difference in how users perceive what is functional or not on a Web page. At Sun's Usability Lab, Jakob Nielsen conducted tests with Sun employees on the design iterations of one of the company's intranets. When the opening page used a flat rectangular button in its design, users passed over the button, thinking it was a decoration. When the button was revised and given an affordance, usage increased by 416 percent over a two-month period.[12]

Version B, by contrast, has little regard for supporting users' tasks. Shneiderman's menu design principles are clearly ignored. Tasks are listed in a frame to the left. Their functionality is minimized by the design: The headings do not have underlined links or any other graphical elements that would help draw users' attention to them, and the lack of contrast and a decorative font style decreases the page's readability. The ordering of the functions is also poorly organized. The first selection in the list reads "About Us." This ordering scheme is more company-centered than user-centered. With Version B, users will have to sort through and try to figure out where the news link is. In this case, the page becomes more of a scavenger hunt page than a site for information retrieval. Users' processing time will undoubtedly increase. For first-time or casual users, the meanings of the headings on the bulleted list may be difficult to figure out and to differentiate from one another. Where is the news link? In Version B, news is linked from the "Happenings," which is a murky translation for "news." The semantic trouble continues with the headings. The heading "Morgue" on the final button is old-fashioned newspaper jargon for a News Library. Most users—even if they are avid Dashiell Hammett fans—are unlikely to make the metaphorical leap. In fact, some users may misinterpret that the heading is a link to obituaries, a popular item that many newspaper sites include.

The point is that task support is fundamental to user-centered design. When an interface supports users' basic tasks, information-processing time is reduced and user satisfaction brims. Over a longer period of time, users' productivity levels are enhanced. It cannot be emphasized enough: Design that supports users' tasks is a significant factor in increasing users' satisfaction levels.

functionality well, the following questions should be asked when looking at the opening screens of any interface:

- Are the functions easy to locate on the screen?

- Do the functions that receive top billing support users or the developer or the company?

- Are the functions easy to read?

- Are the names for functions easy to comprehend?

- Is decision making for users enhanced or impeded by the design?

Usability

Just how *intuitive* is an interface? Interfaces with intuitive designs are ones that allow users to easily and naturally interpret what they are supposed to do. In other words, intuitive sites are usable ones. Typically, users decide within minutes of first interacting with a system whether an interface is usable or not. Besides its literal meaning, usability, from an HCI perspective, addresses the following aspects:[13]

- Is the interface easy to learn?

- Is the interface easy to remember?

- Is the interface pleasant to use?

- Does the interface design cause few errors?

When it comes to evaluating the usability of an interface, consistency is a crucial factor. Consistency has several dimensions in interface design. In particular, consistency concerns the sameness in layout, command names, and graphic vocabulary throughout an entire product. A consistent interface reduces the severity of users' learning curves. Once users learn and are able to remember what and where basic functions are, such as search, print, and quit, they can apply the knowledge that is used throughout their entire interaction experience. Consistency eases learning and navigation, freeing users to concentrate on their tasks. To evaluate the consistency of an interface, the following questions should be asked when looking at a succession of screens in an interface:

- Are fundamental menu functions in the same location from screen to screen, such as print, help, quit, and search?

- Are the same fundamental functions available from screen to screen?

- Is there a semantic clarity in the vocabulary that is used to describe functions, features, and icons from screen to screen?

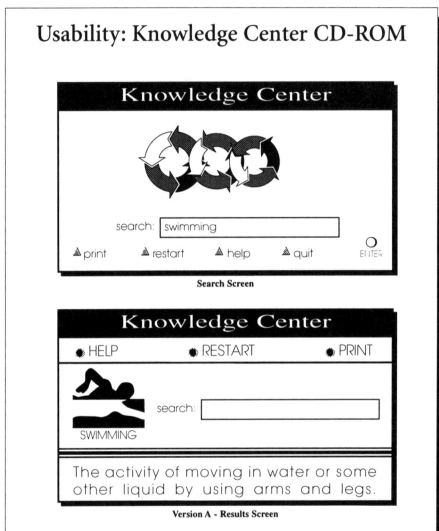

Figure 3.2A Usability—Two Views of the **Knowledge Center** *CD-ROM*

Figures 3.2A and 3.2B show views of a search and results screen for two versions of *Knowledge Center,* a hypothetical homework helper for students on CD-ROM. Which version appears more usable?

The answer is Version B. As the search and results sequence of the two pages shows, Version B provides the user with the same menu, in the same location, from page to page. The logic applied in the design of Version B is

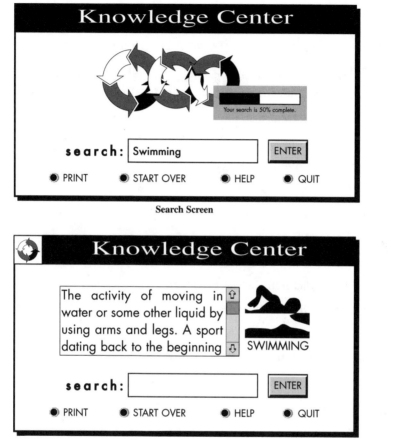

Figure 3.2B Usability—Two Views of the **Knowledge Center** *CD-ROM*

that once the first screen is learned, the same knowledge can be applied on the second screen and throughout. Another usability strength in Version B is the feedback box that appears in the search screen. From the message, users know that the program is processing their search, while giving them a percentage of the amount of processing that has occurred. For beginners and casual users, feedback is an important usability feature because users often have uncertainties when they use systems that are new to them: Is the program working? Did I break the system? What is going on with the processing?

Version A, by contrast, lacks consistency. On the second page of Version A, only the "Help," "Restart," and "Print" button are carried forward from the search screen. The rest of the menu items have disappeared. For new users, this design of Version A can be disorienting. Most users will face a steeper learning curve with Version A; more memorization of individual pages will be an obstacle for regular users. Frustration and memory overload among end users is reduced when a design has consistency. In fact, findings from several HCI experimental research projects indicate that the need for repetitious hands-on training is curtailed by as much as 300 percent when consistent design is used for basic functions and features.[14] Also consider this: If users want to quit the application, there is no direct, easy procedure. To quit Version A, users will have to either turn the machine off or they will need to go back to the opening screen and choose the quit function.

Consistency matters in this example because the CD-ROM is an information retrieval tool for beginning users. However, in recent years, there has been debate in the HCI community about consistency in design. Some authors have argued that as a user becomes more familiar with a system, the need for consistency gives way to more of a need for flexibility, especially with complex functions that may not be characterized by the same sequential and linear characteristics.[15] Reva Basch (who is interviewed at the end of this chapter) addresses the limitations of consistency across applications in her comments about online commercial providers. Arguably, there is a design trade-off with consistency. With low-level menu functions such as searching, quitting, and printing, consistent design is important because it gives users familiarity and processing speed, but with high-level functions, such as storing results in a portfolio file for future use, the need may not be as great.

• Overall, does the interface feel like a single interface or does interacting with the system feel like working with more than one system because of the design variability from screen to screen?

Aesthetics

From an HCI design standpoint, aesthetics deals with the use of color, icons, images, multimedia, and the layout of elements. Visuals matter because they affect users and their attention, comprehension, and ability to read a screen's content. The HCI principle about aesthetics holds that interfaces should communicate visually, helping users absorb information and carry out the tasks they need to do. On the most basic level, an interface's visual elements should impart information, minimize information overload, and manage a user's attention. When it comes to the design of information retrieval resources, less is better. In particular, color and visual elements should be used sparingly so that users can more easily concentrate on information retrieval tasks. Their minimal use lessens the effects of splintered and divided attention. Shneiderman has a well-acknowledged design rule for color. He suggests that each screen should offer no more than four colors to effectively manage users' attention and minimize the effects of clutter.[16] The effective guidance of users' attention is the goal of visual design. When graphical elements are used appropriately, they can sharpen users' ability to prioritize tasks and process information, guiding them through their tasks. Just as landmarks help people navigate in the physical world, design landmarks such as icons, menu bars, and site maps, help users navigate the virtual landscape. To evaluate whether interfaces properly manage a user's attention with visual elements, the following questions should be asked:

• How long does it take to process information appearing on the screen? Do graphical elements help or hinder processing?

Aesthetics: *Business Profiler* Web Page

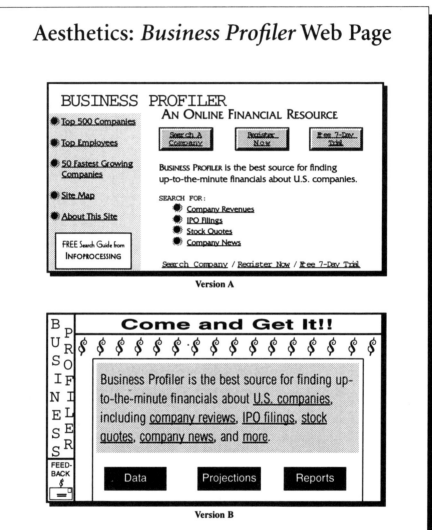

Version A

Version B

Figure 3.3   Aesthetics—Two Views of the Business Profiler *Web Page*

Figure 3.3 shows two versions of *Business Profiler*, a hypothetical Web site used for business research. Which Web page has visual elements that help information processing?

The answer is Version A. Version A carefully directs users' attention toward what is important on the page and what is not. In other words, the visual design subtlely prioritizes the page's content. Contrast and other visual elements (e.g., buttons) are not used to decorate the site but to enhance information processing activities. Functional areas are shaded, links are clearly set apart from one another and have link phrases, not just one word, fully underlined. Also, the font is readable and easy for users to process. The font is also consistently used throughout the page so that readability is enhanced. An advertisement is boxed and placed inconspicuously in the left-hand corner so it does not distract or "fool" users. The guiding design rule applied in Version A is to let users get in and out of the page quickly.

The design of Version B, by contrast, is downright jarring. The bannered advertisement that reads, "Come and Get It!!" is assaulting, distracting, and confusing. At first glance, the user might ask if the ad is part of the site's content or a separate ad. The contrast effect is applied unevenly and illogically, so that it is decorative instead of helping users' information processing tasks. Even though color (contrast here since it is a black and white reproduction) can be a very powerful interface element, users often respond viscerally to it. When color is used effectively, contrast or shading can pull users' attention to certain relevant artifacts on the screen, such as the start button, reducing search time. In Version B, however, the contrast effect is a source of confusion. Another problem is that the underlined links in the body of the page are embedded in the text. The links are both difficult to read and to physically locate as a target with a mouse. The word choice of the headings on the bottom black buttons are broad, vague, and unhelpful. Users will need to do some exploring on their own, diving into the depths of the links, to find out the content that is behind each one of the buttons. Another eyesore is the nearly incomprehensible letter icon in the left-hand corner of the page. The small image is redundant, since the actual word "feedback" appears right above it. In general, the site is cluttered. But the worse example of clutter may be the "$" icon, which is needlessly repetitive and does little to give the site any branding. A simple logo, applied once, would have gone a lot further for creating a visual landmark that could be carried from page to page. Overall, clutter works against users, confusing them about which action to take and overloading their memory capabilities.

- Are graphical elements—color, layout, icons, fonts—used to prioritize key processing information?

- Are users overwhelmed by screens because of an overuse of color? (A standard rule of thumb is no more than four different colors per screen.)

- Do multimedia features—animation and sound—enhance or distract information processing?

The Design Template

Throughout the years, guides have been published for interface designers. Many of them, including the one excerpted below, give good design pointers, such as these:

- Orient the user by providing an overview of the program functions

- Lead the user step by step through standard sequences and operations

- Anticipate the user's next request or need

- Warn the user of potential problems and errors

- Keep the user focused on the current task by eliminating distractions and providing feedback

- Make users feel they are in control

• Provide the environment users want

• Encourage users to exploit the software without fear[17]

Even though this guide excerpt (and many others like it) puts users at center stage, the recommendations are clearly written *by designers for designers*. The guidelines' greatest use for application is during the design and building process, as designers wrangle with the countless design trade-offs they will face. In this book, we have continually drawn from guidelines like these, and from HCI findings, to describe the essentials of good design. But these guidelines are best applied as recipes for the decision making that goes into robust interface building. An approach to assessing and evaluating, instead of carrying out, good design could benefit from its own method in addition to these prescribed guideline specifications.

In this section, we present a design evaluation template in Table 3.2 (which begins on page 62) that has been developed *by users and for users*. The design template is a hands-on guide for assessing existing interfaces from a users' point of view. The goal is to give evaluators key questions to consider about task support, usability, and aesthetics. There is no way the template can anticipate every pro or con about design that readers might uncover in their own testing. What we have tried to give readers are crucial design basics that form a framework for understanding design and user interaction of interfaces, used primarily for information retrieval. There are undoubtedly questions that every evaluator should ask about cost, availability, and content that are far beyond the scope of this template or the book. The intent is to give readers a practical template to apply to evaluation in the field.

Up Ahead

In part 2, individual design analyses of popular information retrieval resources are provided. The analyses work off the basics of the design

Table 3.2 Design Evaluation Template

TASK SUPPORT

Principle:
The interface should meet user expectations and
support the tasks users need to get done.

ISSUE	FOCUS	WHAT TO ASK
Who is the tool for?	*Audience*	• Is this tool a good fit for users' levels of expertise and the job at hand? • Is there design flexibility to accommodate both inexperienced and experienced users? • Does the interface's model of what it is and how it works come close to users' own perceptions?
What do users want to accomplish?	*User Goals*	• What kind of work does the interface support? • Is this the kind of work users will regularly use the interface for? • Is productivity enhanced by using this tool? • How much time does it take to complete a task?

What can users do?	*Functionality*	• Do users have any idea from the opening screens what the interface can do?
		• If the interface has a searching function:
		    Is there truncation?
		    Boolean searching?
		    Search status?
		    Search history displays?
		• What is the general output like?
		• Can users download in a few easy steps?
		• Are other formats supported?
		• How thorough is the record display?
		• Can users customize the display to meet their needs?

Who is in charge?	*Control*	• Who does most of the work—users or the interface? • How flexible is the interface: Do users get to choose when to do what or does the interface exert control over users? • Does the interface help users crystallize their thoughts? • Are users' next requests or needs anticipated? • Who do the design trade-offs favor?

DESIGN WISE A GUIDE FOR EVALUATING THE INTERFACE DESIGN OF INFORMATION RESOURCES
By Alison J. Head, Information Today© 1999.

evaluation template provided in Table 3.2. The analyses focus on
information retrieval resources, in general. There is a chapter devoted to the
design analysis of CD-ROMs, Web sites, and online commercial providers.
The chapter on Web sites also includes a section on design for users with

Table 3.2 Design Evaluation Template continued

USABILITY

Principle:
The interface should be easy to learn, easy to remember, pleasant to use, and cause few errors.

ISSUE	FOCUS	WHAT TO ASK
Is there an ease of use?	*Learnability*	• Is the interface intuitive? • Is there a consistency in layout, graphic vocabulary, and commands? • Are the functions that users need the most displayed prominently(i.e., begin, print, execute, search, display, escape, and quit)? • Does the interface deliver any immediate rewards? • Does the interface avoid frustrating users?
Can users find their way around?	*Navigation*	• How complex is the navigational system? • Can users get through the system quickly? • Is the navigational layout obvious? • Are there visual cues showing what is operational? • Are users' steps retraceable? • Are there too many repetitive steps to move through to get a task done? • Can users customize to eliminate steps?

How helpful is help?	*Assistance*	• Does the interface help users solve problems and cope with mistakes?
		• Is there a break or stop button?
		• Is there a help system that is continuously available?
		• If so, can it help answer questions
		   —directly and simply
		   —about what the program does?
		• Describe what something is for?
		• Tell how an action is carried out?
		• Explain why something happened?
		• Help users navigate if their mental mapping breaks down?
		• Is help proactive, warning users against potential problems?

DESIGN WISE A GUIDE FOR EVALUATING THE INTERFACE DESIGN OF INFORMATION RESOURCES
By Alison J. Head, Information Today© 1999.

special needs, an often neglected area of interface design. Together, the template and the analyses will enable readers to make better decisions about products and services by knowing questions to ask and by understanding how each resource works as an information retrieval tool.

Table 3.2 Design Evaluation Template continued

AESTHETICS

Principle:
The interface should communicate visually, helping users absorb information and carry out the tasks they need to do while minimizing information overload.

ISSUE	FOCUS	WHAT TO ASK
How does the interface look?	*Appearance*	• Is the design a good match with the medium? • Is the attention of users focused or splintered by the use of color and layout? • Does the design take advantage of natural mapping? • Is the screen uncluttered? • How many windows can be opened at once and does this cause any overload? • Is the typography (size and font) effectively used? • Is it readable? • Is color evenly used to prevent clutter and confusion? • Can the interface be customized for users with disabilities?
What is the interface like to use?	*Interaction*	• As users improve at using the interface are more advanced options available? • Do users feel directly engaged when they interact with the tool or is it slow and dragging? • Does the processing speed match that of users? • If there is sound, is it irritating and, if so, can it be turned off? • How many keystrokes does it take to carry out a task? • Is the processing time worth it? • Could the tool exacerbate repetitive stress injuries?
Are we having fun yet?	*Enjoyment*	• Does the tool delight? • Is a level of interest maintained? • Do users get what they want done now? • Does the tool encourage users to jump ahead, rather than click on the same path? • Is the response time reasonable? • Is this a tool worth having?

DESIGN WISE A GUIDE FOR EVALUATING THE INTERFACE DESIGN OF INFORMATION RESOURCES
By Alison J. Head, Information Today© 1999.

Table 3.3 The Pick of the Lot: Recommended Readings

Raymond W. Crow and Robert F. Starbird, "Easier Said than Done: Practical Considerations in User Interface Design," *Government Information Quarterly*, vol. 9. no. 2, 1992, pp. 169–85.

Hal P. Kirkwood, Jr., "Beyond Evaluation: A Model for Cooperative Evaluation of Internet Resources," *ONLINE*, vol. 22, no. 4, July–August, 1998, pp. 66–72.

David Shenk, *Data Smog: Surviving Information Glut*, San Francisco: Harper Edge, 1997.

INSIDE . . .

An Interview with Reva Basch About Information Industry Changes

Reva Basch is the author of Researching Online for Dummies *(1998) and* Secrets of the Super Net Searchers *(1996), editor of the "Super Searchers" book series, as well as a columnist for* ONLINE *magazine, and a well-known information industry expert.*

How would you characterize the information explosion that is occurring?

It's not so much that there is a great quantity of information in the world in an absolute sense. What is going on is that there is information impinging on us and knocking on our consciousness in a much more direct and overlookable way. Access is what has changed.

So what's happening is really an access explosion instead of an information explosion?

Yes. Visibility and search options are what are exploding.

How does all of this affect people, in general, who are looking for information?

The changes are creating a lot of fear, uncertainty, and anxiety. Partly because there is so much information there, but partly because of the choices and the varieties of possible pathways in online environments. Most people, putting aside information professionals who have been working with information for a long time, are very uncomfortable with the online environment. Most people are struggling with the medium at the same time that they are trying to find their way through the maze of content.

With all the information out there, does someone like you even feel overwhelmed?

All of the time! I have a pile of magazines upstairs, most of which are information-industry related. I am trying to figure out which of these is going to be my best information filter. Are any of my print subscriptions superior to the online updates that I subscribe to? Which of the online updates are doing me any good at all? It's insane. We all rely on whatever our filtering mechanism is; having some kind of filter has become essential. I know my filtering mechanism operates more hours per day than it is used to; part of that is a function of online now being twenty-four hours a day, seven days a week, which it never used to be. It used to be that you would dial up Dow Jones or Nexis-Lexis during the workday; however, since we are using online for so much more now than just information gathering, it has become all-pervasive.

What about information product developers and designers—are they doing anything to help?

It depends on where you look. Search engine designers, for instance, certainly don't seem to be helping. Instead, engine developers are driven very much by marketing considerations. I think it is with AltaVista that, when you do a search, the first hit you get has actually paid so that they can appear at the top of your hit lists. Goto.com is another example of purely a pay-for-placement service. It is frightening to think that your search results are dependent, essentially, on what an advertiser has chosen to do. But then at the same time, there are certain sites and services that are positioning themselves as the answer to infoglut; Northern Light being one. One thing that is helpful that is happening on the Web is the channelization of information—the subject approach that we're seeing on search engines like Excite.

In the last 10 years, how has "the optimal interface" for information research work changed and with what consequences?

Command-based interfaces used to be the tool. There used to be a certain machismo about just seeing that question mark alone on the screen, like when you used Dialog, and actually knowing what to do with it. You could almost feel the force of the machine on the other end. It typed back at you, you typed in, it typed back. You had to know these arcane commands. Now, I think we have sacrificed a lot with graphical user interfaces, which has become the optimal interface for most. For as long as I had a choice, I refused GUI versions on every online service that I used. Initially, I had strong feelings that they were just too cute, I didn't need pretty pictures, I needed text. GUIs were, and still are, slower to navigate. Not only is there a slowness in physical response time, but also when traversing a screen with your mouse. But it is funny, because now with GUIs, I often do feel immersed in the work environment.

When it comes to evaluating information resources, what has changed?

None of these sources are standing still, which makes evaluation especially hard. Not only is it overwhelming, the environment is vastly dynamic. I always laugh when people ask me about what I think the best search engine is. In my own evaluation, what I try to do is to point people toward criteria for judging performance quality; I give them suggestive approaches. You might not want to start with a search engine, you may want to start with subject guides, like Yahoo! I may point them to a megasite that I know someone reliable has put together. Or, I may try to give them some criteria, some questions to ask such as: Who has put the tool together? When was it last updated? How current is it? How substantial? How real is it?

Standards for evaluation have changed because the interface, as we know it, has changed so much. We now have the Web. Issues about pricing have certainly changed. With the Web there's a trade-off, pricing is not a hot button anymore, but waiting to get the information is! The idea of the graceful interface is important now. We never worried in the early days about non-intuitive commands. It was more of a case of commercial online providers selling us subscriptions and saying here are the commands—memorize them! So what we wanted then was a common command language. We wanted all of the text-based systems to emulate each other, until we realized that what that would mean would be settling for the lowest common denominator. We would lose specialized commands because the commands couldn't be easily mapped to the competition. There was a degree of warranty that was much more dependent on your skill as a searcher. You got better as a searcher, but the interface did not get better. The big change with GUIs is that even though you may discover shortcuts, you are pretty much locked into whatever design is there.

Endnotes

1. Stephen Buel, "Business Leap Ahead on Net: The Trend Could Boost Economy and Reshape Some U.S. Industries," *San Jose Mercury News*, April 16, 1998, p. 1A.
2. Anonymous, "Tremble Everyone," *The Economist*, May 10, 1997, pp. E10–3.
3. "Amazon.com Seeks to Triple Shares," *San Jose Mercury News*, April 19, 1998, p. E16.
4. Donna Carvajal, "Online Bookstores Do Battle," *New York Times*, March 17, 1998, p. E1.
5. "Tremble Everyone," op. cit., p. E10.

6. For more on information glut and deluge, see David Shenk, *Data Smog, San Francisco*: Harper Edge, 1997.

7. Raymond W. Crow, and Robert F. Starbird, "Easier Said than Done: Practical Considerations in User Interface Design," *Government Information Quarterly*, vol. 9. no. 2, 1992, p. 172.

8. Gitta Salomon, "New Uses of Color," In Brenda Laurel, ed. *The Art of Human-Computer Interface Design*, Reading, Mass.: Addison-Wesley Publishing Company, 1990, pp. 269–78.

9. Ibid.

10. G. A. Miller, "The Magical Number Seven Plus or Minus Two: Some Limits on Our Capacity for Processing Information," *Psychological Review*, vol. 63, 1956, pp. 81–97.

11. Ben Shneiderman, *Designing the User Interface: Strategies for Effective Human-Computer Interaction*, Reading, Mass.: Addison-Wesley Publishing Company, 1993.

12. Jakob Nielsen, "Usability Testing of WWW Designs," Sun Microsystems Web site. Available http://www.sun.com/sun-on-net/uidesign. 19 Feb. 1999. Search by title to get directly to source.

13. Jakob Nielsen, *Multimedia and Hypertext: The Internet and Beyond*, Boston: AP Professional, 1995, p. 281.

14. P. Polson, "The Consequences of Consistent and Inconsistent User Interfaces," In Raymond Guindon, ed. *Cognitive Science and Its Applications for Human-Computer Interaction*, Hillsdale, N.J.: Erlbaum, 1988.

15. Jonathan Grudin, "The Case Against User Interface Consistency," *Communications of the ACM*, vol. 32, no. 10, Oct. 1989, pp. 1164–73.

16. Shneiderman, op. cit., p. 98.

17. James E. Powell, *Designing User Interfaces*, San Marcos, Calif.: Microtrend, 1990, pp. 16–7.

Note: Date following Web citations indicates date of access.

Part 2

INTERFACE DESIGN ANALYSES

4 CD-ROMs: Treasure Trove or Wasteland?

ven with the advent of the Web, CD-ROMs have managed to hold onto their slot as popular information resources. The sustenance of the CD market is one sure sign of its vitality. The number of available titles only continues to grow, increasing a thousand-fold since an initial offering of 48 titles in 1986.[1] For the most part, CD-ROM information resources—encyclopedias, dictionaries, and citation and content databases—have had particular success in securing loyal users with products that deliver full text. In schools and libraries, users strongly prefer CDs over print sources when carrying out research because CDs are considered easier, more efficient, and more accessible than their print counterparts.[2] And for institutions facing the persistent problems of space and money, CD-ROMs can be a panacea. Large amounts of data can be stored in multimedia formats, the cost is affordable, little space is needed for storage, and the networking potential of CDs creates resources for sharing, giving users twenty-four-hour access, seven days a week. Both user and institutional support have earned CDs a reputation as highly sought-after resources.

Design Analysis
Task Support: The Big Lie

CD-ROMs are strangely paradoxical resources. In many cases, the tasks CDs are designed to support tend to be grossly mismatched with how they

Design in a Nutshell

CD-ROMs are marketed as the quintessential end-user resource because of an implied ease of use. But evaluators should know that CD interfaces can be deceptively simple. In fact, CDs often look so easy to use that users think they do not need any training at all. This just is not true. There are several design factors that can make CDs a fundamentally difficult resource for end users to ever fully master. Beginning with task support, CDs can be contradictory devices. Souped-up with functions that many users will never comprehend let alone use, CDs are undeniably underutilized resources. When users are met with screens offering far too many options, they typically *dumb down* search tasks. There is a strange irony with research CD-ROMs: Most users perform simplified searches that turn out less-than-appropriate results, yet many of the same users still are satisfied with their search results.

The source of many usability problems is rooted in the diversity of CD-ROM design. The rapid success of the multimedia industry has spawned CDs that lack standardization and consistency across products. What users have learned in one CD—which functions are named and where they appear on the screen—may not apply in the next disc they use. CD jukeboxes that house multiple CDs, a common setup in many library settings, are rife with confusion for users plagued by a variety of discs that require constant relearning. Under these conditions, users are left without transferable skills from one application to the next. Information professionals are guaranteed increases in hands-on training.

Unfortunately, CDs can behave like a wallflower at a junior high dance: Neither makes the first move. Users are expected to dive into CDs with little instruction and take the initiative. Prompts that guide users to the next logical action are an important design interaction component that is frequently absent. Feedback—messages that communicate whether the system is processing users' actions—can also be minimal. If processing takes a long time and users are not alerted that their request is being handled, users (especially beginners) assume that the system has crashed, and they walk away. In addition to all of this, CDs may require multiple steps to get to basic functions such as searching and printing, which only serve to increase processing time. Under all of these conditions, both novices and casual users tend to flounder.

Finally, the multimedia of CD-ROM research tools can get in the way of users' efforts to absorb information. Cluttered screens, a multitude of overlapping windows, and poorly executed sound effects impair how users' attention gets focused and managed. When interacting with this kind of interface, users' capacity for learning and memorizing a system is greatly impeded, especially if a CD is set up in a work environment that is noisy, busy, and distracting. Despite their design limitations, CDs have survived and in some instances even prospered in the wake of the Web. Even though their search features tend to be underutilized, CDs have strengths as information retrieval resources that come from their tangible quality and their finite content.

actually end up being used. Part of the discrepancy arises from users' perceptions about CDs. Users see a CD as a friendly tool that supports very basic information retrieval tasks. As a result, most users never plumb the full depths of CD search features, reaping only half-hearted citations that expert researchers would regularly rebuff.[3] One study of college students' use of CDs in an academic library showed that more than one-third of the citations retrieved were inappropriate and useless for the topic they were actually trying to research.[4] This finding about CDs, which appeared in a library and information science journal, is not uncommon. The reason for the incongruity between CD capabilities and users' exploitation can be partially explained by the varying levels of searching proficiency among users. Still, interface design inadequacies play a large part in why some CDs fail to support users, their tasks, and their skill levels.

Before the shrink wrap even comes off, many CDs have already started to convey the wrong message about the level of searchers that the tool is really designed to support. CDs are regularly packaged as user-friendly, mainstream resources sold by vendors who tout a medium requiring little, if any, training. Instead, CDs are actually design hybrids that try to be *all things to all levels of users*, both beginners and experts. One author has argued that, among beginners, CDs in general create a "false confidence syndrome," and that "CD-ROM users find these products to be so easy to search that they feel no need for instruction on their use."[5] Many librarians have learned the lesson about CD training the hard way.

A recent study of CD users in an academic library showed that even though nearly three-quarters of the sample (489 respondents) considered themselves confident at searching twenty-two different CD-ROM databases, one-third still wanted to become more effective searchers, especially when it came to searching multiple databases.[6] The study revealed that users wanted training through personal assistance from staff or at least from hands-on workshops. The authors concluded that "ironically, hands-on training at the point of need is the most costly, most time-consuming, and most demanding of reference staff."[7] For evaluators considering CDs for an organizational setting, it is important to note that the money that CDs may save initially could end up being doled out for user training.

From a design evaluation viewpoint, CDs are rarely, if ever, a plug-and-play technology. The majority of users' efforts go into working out the basic functions of CDs. Users may have little chance to move from the conceptual (figuring out) to the procedural (doing tasks) level.[8] CD menus exemplify the point. There are three common organizing principles for the design of full-screen menus, which are based on expected frequency of use, logical sequence of operations, and alphabetical ordering.[9] Because CD workstations tend to be accessed by many users, the interface should order options by logical sequence, meaning the relevancy of when the task is carried out. To the contrary, many developers confuse relevance with abundance and variety. Subsequently, users may see a logical sequence of menu items, but they often end up being overloaded by the number of available options they see on one screen. When met with too many choices to process, users tend to search through the fields and select the lowest common denominator. Users figure their selection will deliver some results, no matter how imprecise.

Usability: A Horse of a Different Color

The CD market has grown willy-nilly over the past 20 years, delivering a multitude of differing products and a legacy of usability problems in its commercial wake. In a nutshell, CDs lack a standardized design in three far-reaching common areas: (1) There is a dearth of standardized retrieval software on which CDs can run; (2) there is a variety of interface platforms for CDs (i.e., graphical user interfaces versus DOS-based systems versus Web interactive versions); and (3) there is great variability in the design consistency among individual products. The wide diversity of CD technology makes evaluation rife with confusion. It is not unusual for institutions to develop a collection of CDs that is as idiosyncratic as a seashell collection from a summer vacation at the beach. The Western Ontario Library System, for instance, subscribes to 40 different CD-ROM titles, which run on 22 different software packages.[10] Any design evaluation of CD-ROM products must also involve an assessment of consistency within individual interfaces as well as the wider contexts of the software package the CD runs on and, ultimately, the resource environment within which the CD will be placed. As the following product field test shows, a newly developed CD-ROM feature, Web interactivity, makes questions of consistency even more challenging.

Field Test:
Grolier Multimedia Encyclopedia

Encyclopedias are a starting point, the student's first recourse for getting the scope of a topic or an overview that should suggest paths for further research. It would seem that the new Internet outlinks from Grolier Multimedia Encyclopedia (GME) would be the main advantage over a print encyclopedia, the feature that justifies the medium. Unfortunately, in this field test, Web interactivity turned out to be the most frustrating part of using GME. Here's an account of what happened.

Before I begin searching, I need to install the discs. Two discs: a bad sign. Swapping them in and out may be a problem (though I never did manage to reach Disc 2 and find out). But there is a good sign: fat documentation, a 32-page booklet for using the CD. However, I bet most end users go full-speed ahead without it, checking instructions only when they are at a dead end. Even though the booklet claims "installation will begin automatically," it does not. It is a struggle even with prior experience. The installation of the included QuickTime program is easy. Getting the sample movie to play is not. There is no start button or other affordance that gives a visual cue for functionality. Nothing is mentioned about installing an Internet browser, which I know I will need for future interactivity. CDs have been criticized for their lack of prompts that help get users going, and this is an example of where prompts are most needed. The completed installation has not created the shortcut program icon that the instructions implied. I have to find GME in the Programs area, and it's three directories deep. This takes extra time.

A musical chord confirms that the sound works, without delaying the start of the program. (One competitor encyclopedia actually starts with a long theme song that cannot be turned off.) A busy, dark collage background makes the screen feel cramped at first, but the layout—table of contents frame at left, contents frame at right, toolbar at bottom, and feature bar at top—is familiar to me from Web conventions. Still, the visuals leave users with a lot to process at first, when in most cases, they may be trying to focus on how to get one task—searching—done.

What to search? Belly dance is a subject that cries out for multimedia, and one I know has a wealth of Web resources. But GME gives it only one brief unattributed paragraph, with no bibliography or illustrations of the dance, let alone any related articles, movies, or Web links. The sound sample is illustrated only with a view of the Bosphorus. If I hoped for a starting point for research, this would stop me dead in my tracks. I decide to use the "complex" search option, which offers Boolean in an easy-to-use template but does not mention the availability of truncation or wildcards. A search for "dance" AND "middle east" OR "arab*" brought up 996 possibilities, in no apparent order, many with only one of the required terms. There are too many results to sort through and no apparent way to refine the search in progress. Choosing one of the results at random (Jimmy Carter's Camp David speech), I discover that search terms are marked by underlining (the standard for a hyperlink, though links here are blue and not underlined) and there is no "find in page" or "find next" feature to save me scrolling time when I try to locate the next keyword.

The article on Arabian music (found in the browse list) is much longer, signed, and has a bibliography, an "Outline" pop-up, and an Internet link. My browser is already open, but the Internet connection did not bring it to the front or open a new window on top of the GME, as my experience with other programs led me to expect. I assume the system has failed. Because the GME fills the whole screen, it hides the Win95 status bar (extremely unsettling), so there is no feedback on what windows are open. Alt-tabbing out to Notepad, I find the Internet window open, but with a "timed out" message for every attempt I had made. If this is a matter of server overload between 4:00 PM and 9:00 PM, which are prime homework hours, usability for students is seriously diminished.

Another try, late that night, when the server should be free: With the browser not yet open, I get a message "to choose and install browser under Preferences." This never came up during the installation, nor when I first fired up the program. Does GME assume all users have the integrated program suites that automatically open a browser? I eventually connect to a general resource on music and a music vendor with bad frames. The next GME outlink I try appears in that page's center frame; I close the browser and try again.

So far, GME is fun to browse (for the unlikely topics listed) but frustrating to use as an information retrieval tool. Results are not always on-topic, they cannot be refined, and the Web links meant to augment the content may not be reachable. The biggest costs to users using this resource for information retrieval are processing time and searching precision. GME, especially the Web interactivity, needs some more work to make it a worthwhile information resource from the user's point of view.

Field testing of Grolier Multimedia Encyclopedia 1998 (Version 10.0 for Windows 95) was performed and written by Jo Falcon, San Jose State University Graduate School of Library and Information Science, during the first two weeks of August, 1998.

In all fairness, even before the lure of Web interactivity, there were inherent problems associated with CD-ROM usability. In fact, the design inconsistencies drove a group of information professionals to call for more standards, especially in the areas of terminology and functionality. In 1992, the Special Interest Group on CD-ROM Applications and Technology (SIGCAT) released CD design guidelines in response to the "ever increasing assortment of software interfaces and command sets being used for

---

Table 4.1 SIGCAT Design Principles for CD-ROMs

• Consistency of triggers and prompts throughout

• Provisions for error handling and easy reversal of actions

• Flexibility of design, accommodating novices and experts

• Continuous availability of Help and Quit and display of these functions in the same place throughout

• Standardization of all functions. Functions always listed in the same order. Standard operation of navigation

• Keep user informed of what is happening or what is required

---

Source: E. J. McFaul, "CD-ROM Consistent Interface Guidelines: A Final Report," *CD-ROM Librarian*, vol. 7, no. 2, Feb. 1993, p. 26.

CD-ROMs."[11] There was a call for uniformity in naming conventions (i.e., help, browse, index, search, display, print, download, restart, change, quit, execute, break, and escape), their ordering, and their placement on the screen.[12] The SIGCAT developed guidelines for top level searching, operational commands, navigational support, and ergonomics. The SIGCAT also recommended essential design principles, which appear in Table 4.1 and are still relevant for evaluating today's CD products.[13]

Péter Jacsó (who is interviewed at the end of this chapter) admits that the SIGCAT guidelines that appear in Table 4.1 did not make the impression with the producers that the information professionals were anticipating. Nevertheless, some CD-ROM suppliers now make the same suite of CD-ROM products available in several versions of standardized software. Still, however, there is great variability in individual CD interfaces, especially in terms of the products' terminology. What one program calls *browse*, for instance, another may call *expand*.

Usability—an ease in learning and retaining interface functionality—may first become an issue for users when they access a CD-ROM jukebox. In academic libraries, undergraduates often bring a conceptual model to the interaction exchange, basing what they know on a general purpose CD-ROM from their high school, public library, and/or promotional product bundling from a home personal computer.[14] When undergraduates are first faced with the onslaught of specialized subject databases, the users (like most any others) are likely to either muddle through and gather many inappropriate results, seek hands-on assistance, and/or learn one CD out of the stack and use it for everything. A library worker I spoke with about CD-ROM use recently told me of a student who was an avid user of MEDLINE, the National Library of Medicine's information source that is available from a number of CD vendors. Every paper the student researched and wrote during her four years at the university was based on research pulled from MEDLINE. In fact, the student even wrote a paper for her political science class using MEDLINE! Unfortunately, the story confirms an unfavorable interface design adage: Users will eventually learn to adapt their needs to any design, whether or not the resource is a good fit.

Usability problems can only worsen when users try to perform a search. The search interface is an infamous CD-ROM trouble spot. A majority of CDs have retrieval features that are uninteractive, confusing, and unhelpful. CD-ROM users can be expected to dive in and take the initiative. The interface may offer few prompts for guiding users effectively and efficiently through their tasks. Error messages can be incomprehensible. A restart, quit, and help button should appear on every screen, but typically do not. When a search is being carried out, the interface should deliver feedback to users about how many records are being retrieved and how much longer the user needs to wait for final results. With any interface, feedback is a major aspect of a usable design. Users need to know whether they are making progress. The menu bar, a good spot for conveying processing information, is typically underutilized by CD product developers. Navigating through search results can be tremendously powered-down when CDs do not highlight search terms in the text and/or let users jump to the next search term.

For many casual and beginning users, a major limitation can be the shortage of search instructions and examples. Because of the variability among CD products, the lack of searching instructions is a gross oversight, especially for a supposedly user-friendly resource. A related feature is a useful help system. But CD-ROM help systems can overload would-be users with screen after screen of irrelevant content and jargon, or both. Because of the prevalence of beginning users, there is a tremendous need in CD design for context-sensitive help systems. This type of help system feature kicks back concise solutions to the user's actual problem at hand, instead of defaulting to endless listings from which users must select.

Aesthetics: A Slippery Slope

Clutter is the Achilles' heel of CD-ROM design. As we saw in the earlier discussion of task support, clutter can impact menu design and users' ability to efficiently respond to the interface. But clutter can extend beyond the menu, becoming pervasive throughout some CDs, creeping in to greatly impede users' ability to absorb and process information. For developers of CD products, a design trade-off exists between the number of screens that are used to visually convey information and the amount of text that appears on each screen. Less text per screen, a remedy for many clutter problems, means that users will need to click through more screens, which is a sure-fire way to increase users' processing time. Design trade-offs, as this example shows, are not always easily resolved.

The excessive overlay of windows or pull-down menus can also reduce users' capacity for processing information. Many users have attention that is easily diminished; they possess a low tolerance for processing dialog boxes or windows that are progressively stacked on a screen. One early CD-ROM had an overlay of six pull-down menus, which ended up overloading many users.[15] In other cases, CDs have emerging boxes or windows that obscure relevant information on the screen. A viable design solution is to equip windows and boxes with a close or back button. This minor design alteration benefits users, giving them more control over the working environment. Another solution to managing user attention is through the effective and appropriate use of color.

In any medium, color is a powerful design element. Used wisely in CD-ROM design, color can guide users' attention by demarcating hierarchies within menus, highlighting search terms, and identifying fields and sub-fields within records. But used poorly, color can overwhelm users and render them hopelessly confused. There are design rules about the application of color to which many commercial CDs closely adhere. Even in the wake of Web design, which has undoubtedly increased users' tolerance for color, a well-acknowledged standard is that the number of different colors displayed should not exceed four per screen and seven in an entire sequence of screens.[16] When choosing CD information resources, this recommendation is significant. When CDs are used primarily for research, color should not be intrusive or distracting to the information retrieval tasks at hand. Color coding matters, too. Coding should be logical and consistent throughout the interface, corresponding to semantic translations where possible. The color red, for instance, signals danger or warning, while green telegraphs go. Still, color hierarchies are limited; only a few recognizable standards really exist.

There is little written about typography and CDs, even though readability is of prime concern when it comes to any interface. One recommendation for CD design is a mix of upper- and lowercase type because it is easier to read.[17] Unlike the limitations of color hierarchies, typography can often communicate hierarchies to users in a simple way. A larger font over a smaller one can signal relevance to users. The most important design factor with type, however, is that the size can be customized by users to meet a wide range of their needs. Sometimes to compensate for readability, CDs, especially encyclopedias, offer a zoom feature. The zoom, however, has been called a "gimmick" that is regularly used to compensate for poor design that has ineffectively used the screen's real estate.[18]

A final multimedia element is sound. So far, the only way that users appreciate listening to an information resource CD-ROM, however, is when the sound is used sparingly and when it applies directly to what the user sees on the screen. A sound sequence that is incidental to the content is annoying and distracting. A review of *Compton's Multimedia Encyclopedia*, for example, praises its incorporation of the audio of Martin Luther King's "I Have a Dream" speech. However, the use of sound in the same CD for the earthquake entry "sounds like breaking bottles, adds nothing to the understanding of earthquakes, and is unlikely to unnerve the most faint-hearted."[19]

The Point

When CD-ROMs were first ushered into information settings in the mid-1980s, they were embraced as welcome alternatives to microfilm and microfiche. The thin, iridescent discs defined multimedia until the Web came along. In fact, it still is the multimedia aspects of CDs—the images, the video clips, and the sound—that provide a rich interaction to general users that print research resources rarely, if ever, achieve. A recent product review of CD-ROM encyclopedias perfectly captured the gee-whiz effect.

Today we used the *Compton's Interactive World Atlas*, part of the *Compton's Interactive Encyclopedia*, to fly a virtual airplane over the North Pole. Jumping around hyperlinks, pulling up text at the click of the button, and generally following research whim after whim, we could not help but wonder what Pliny the Elder or Denis Diderot, the original encyclopedists, would think about the newest crop of flashy, multimedia encyclopedias.[20]

Even in the long shadows cast by the Web, CDs are an intermediary information resource that can still deliver basic information retrieval methods to users and keep them satisfied. The combination of CD qualities—their fixed, finite content; their predictable multimedia; and their tangibility—has delivered a reprieve, for the time being, to the marketability of CD products. Despite the design limitations mentioned throughout this

---

Table 4.2 CD-ROM Design Evaluation Checklist

- Users are presented with at least two interfaces, simple and advanced, insuring flexibility for users' skill levels (beginner vs. intermediate and expert).

- Consistency exists throughout the CD design's layout, terminology, color, placement, and order of basic functions (print, restart, search, help, and quit) to enhance learnability.

- Menus are comprehensible so that users can make quick decisions and get work accomplished.

- Each screen has restart, quit, and help buttons that are highly visible so that users have quick recovery.

- Prompts about "what to do next" guide users through the interaction process.

- Searching features include Boolean, field searching, and proximity operators, which support all levels of users' skill. Search examples are included.

- Retrieval aids, especially indexing and a thesaurus, are included and are browsable.

- Feedback about users' processing status, especially the number of records found so far and percentage to go during searching, appears so that users know the system is working.

- Search histories can be saved for re-selection and editing to make more efficient use of processing time.

- Search terms are highlighted; users can jump to next context so that navigation and processing time are efficiently managed.

- Customizing options exist for output, download, print formats, font size, screen colors, and record layout to meet users' special needs.

- Menu bars include seven or fewer menu options per screen to limit clutter and help users absorb information.

- Color is used sparingly, making information easy to process.

- Screens are not cluttered and overlapping windows are kept to a minimum (six) so that users' attention is visually managed for task support.

- Font style and size is readable or can be customized to meet the needs of users with disabilities.

- The help system is context-sensitive and concise, and offers step-by-step help so that beginning users can successfully interact with the system.

- Help is available throughout the program by pressing F1, a universal DOS standard for help.

- Error messages are comprehensible so that users do not get stuck.

- Tutorial is available at all times to help users learn the system at any point.

Table 4.3 The Pick of the Lot: Recommended Readings and Web Sites

Victoria Manglano Bosch and Micheline Hancock-Beaulieu, "CD-ROM User Interface Evaluation: The Appropriateness of GUIs," *Online and CDROM Review*, vol. 19, no. 5, 1995, pp. 255–70.

Cheryl A. McCarthy, Sylvia C. Krausse, and Arthur A. Little, "Expectations and Effectiveness Using CD-ROMs: What Do Patrons Want and How Satisfied are They?" *College & Research Libraries*, vol. 58, no. 2, March 1997, pp. 128–42.

Trevor Richards and Christine Robinson, "Evaluating CD-ROM Software: A Model," *CD-ROM Professional*, Sept. 1993, pp. 92–101.

Jennifer Rowley and Frances Slack. "The Evaluation of Interface Design on CD-ROMs," *Online and CD-ROM Review*, vol. 21, no. 1, 1997, pp. 3–13.

The SIGCAT Foundation (Special Interest Group on CD Applications and Technology). Available http://www.sigcat.org.

chapter, many CD-ROMs have interfaces that can satisfy and do engage users. For evaluators, the best CD-ROM picks, however, should be ones that are designed to have consistency and support users' expectations for full-text records and ease of use. A compilation of CD evaluation criteria appears in Table 4.2 (see page 86).[21]

INSIDE . . .

An Interview with Péter Jacsó on Making Choices About CD-ROM Products

Péter Jacsó is an Associate Professor in the Department of Information and Computer Sciences, University of Hawaii at Honolulu. He is a columnist for Information Today *and a regular contributor to* ONLINE *magazine.*

What do people tend to consider when evaluating CDs?

Beyond the content, my impression is that they primarily base their judgment on familiarity with the title, like *Books in Print* on CD or *Dissertation Abstracts*, where the relationship with the print carries a lot of weight in favor of the CD-ROM. Then, and only then, they look at the interface. The primary criteria for any institutional use is familiarity with the title.

What else should these evaluators be looking at, in addition to these things?

There are a couple of things they should be looking at, software is one thing and the content is the other thing. Within the software, you want to consider many things, such as how can you navigate, how can you look up terms, how can you search, how can you define your output, how can you display, how can you print. The interface is a big part of the software, a part that is very crucial to evaluation. Very often if users' first impressions of an interface are not good, it is because the interface itself is not intuitive. "Intuitivity" is the key to good interface design. What I mean by intuitive is that, without any formal training, the user can look at the interface and it makes sense.

What are CD-ROM interfaces particularly good at doing for users?

Most are good at providing a consistent interface to a very large amount of data at one time. For example, I can have a CD-ROM database with four gigabytes of data from one single source and it has one single interface for accessing the whole collection. I can keep doing searches rather than going here, going there, and picking up information by learning an interface each time. For the most part, you don't have to shift gears and change the interface every time you move within the product line. Let me make a comparison. It's like traveling in America versus traveling in Europe: If you are traveling a thousand miles in Europe, then you are in different cultures with different customs with different languages, but in America there is more consistency, wherever you travel. CDs are like traveling in America because there is more consistency.

Have CD-ROM producers responded to guidelines issued by librarians and the SIGCAT for more standardized and consistent design?

No, unfortunately. SIGCAT did a good job of trying to develop guidelines. It's an uphill battle, though. It is one of the most frustrating experiences of mine that the users of the software couldn't agree even on very essential things. Their agreement is not restricted to only CDs, but also to online resources. Rather than waiting for users to have a common command language, there are three systems that use a common command language.

The systems adapt themselves to whatever language the user is using. One example of this is UMI and a relatively unknown feature called alias. Behind the scenes, the system can recognize four or five different field tags. For the tag "journal," the user could put in "jn" or "jo" or "jt," and a dictionary would translate any of these entries into the word "journal."

Where do users get bogged down when interacting with CDs?

Problems begin with more complex databases and queries, especially when users are offered too many search options. It's tough, though, because when you have full-text databases, it is essential that you provide users with positional operators. The public, which is far less interested in these specific details, really gets bogged down by these choices. Many CDs try to provide two different interfaces, one for beginners and one for experts, but sometimes there is an overlap and there is no visible fence built into the design of the interface that instructs beginning users not to cross over the fence because the number of choices can be too much.

Beyond CDs with Web interactivity, will CD-ROMs survive the Web?

CDs will survive because there is still a very large population that doesn't have easy and convenient access to the Internet as we have here in the U.S. And for those people, having something on their desktop is very important. Many institutions, too, still favor CDs because they are tangible. It's like ownership, even though you only license.

Where will CDs be in the year 2000?

There will be further victims of changing times among CDs, and that will include some big names, too. All of a sudden, a very large market of users for CDs has migrated to the Web. In the near future, there will not be a big market, for example, for *Books in Print* on CD, which is produced by Bowker. The big market is based in the U.S., Australia, and Britain. It may not be feasible for Bowker to keep producing CDs for a relatively small market that is elsewhere.

If there is a widely known database out there that is a competitor to *Books in Print*, it is Amazon.com. In nearly every regard, Amazon is *Books in Print*. I'm overwhelmed with how good Amazon is. The site just keeps improving. In a short time Amazon has run circles around *Books in Print* by offering search capabilities and much more. There are at least five different search possibilities with Amazon's interface. When you think about the innovation, the smartness, and the vengeance with which Amazon first appeared, you wonder why none of the online systems ever added any one of these extraordinarily good features. In every regard, Amazon has an intuitive interface design.

Endnotes

1. M. Finlay, ed., *Facts and Figures 1993: CD-ROM and CDs*, London: TFPL Publishing, 1993.
2. Cheryl A. McCarthy, Sylvia C. Krausse, and Arthur A. Little, "Expectations and Effectiveness Using CD-ROMS: What Do Patrons Want and How Satisfied are They?" *College & Research Libraries*, vol. 58, no. 2, March 1997, p. 135.
3. Victoria Manglano Bosch and Micheline Hancock-Beaulieu, "CD-ROM User Interface Evaluation: The Appropriateness of GUIs," *Online & CD ROM Review*, vol. 19, no. 5, 1995, p. 255.
4. Stanley D. Nash and Myoung C. Wilson, "Value-Added Bibliographic Instruction: Teaching Students to Find the Right Citations," *References Services Review*, vol. 19, no. 1, 1991, pp. 87–92.
5. F. W. Lancaster, et al., "Searching Databases on CD-ROM: Comparison of the Results of End-User Searching with Results for Two Modes Searching by Skilled Intermediaries," *Reference Quarterly*, vol. 33, no. 3, 1994, pp. 370–86.
6. McCarthy, Krausse, and Little, op. cit., p. 137.
7. Ibid.
8. Bosch and Hancock-Beaulieu, op. cit., p. 268.
9. Joseph S. Dumas, *Designing User Interface Software*, Englewood Cliffs, N.J.: Prentice-Hall, 1988, p. 69.
10. Trevor Richards and Christine Robinson, "Evaluating CD-ROM Software: A Model," *CD-ROM Professional*, Sept. 1993, p. 96.

11. E. J. McFaul, "CD-ROM Consistent Interface Guidelines: A Final Report," *CD-ROM Librarian*, vol. 7, no. 2, Feb. 1992, p. 18.

12. McFaul, op. cit., p. 26.

13. McFaul, op. cit., p. 26.

14. McCarthy, Krausse, and Little, op. cit., p. 131.

15. Andy Large, "The User Interface to CD-ROM Databases," *Journal of Librarianship and Information Science*, vol. 23, no. 4, Dec. 1991, p. 213.

16. Ben Shneiderman, *Designing the User Interface: Strategies for Effective Human-Computer Interaction*, Reading, Mass.: Addison-Wesley Publishing Company, 1993, p. 338.

17. Large, op. cit., p. 213.

18. Ibid.

19. Large, op. cit., p. 214.

20. Barbara Burg, "Virtual Knowledge: The Best Buys in 1998 CD-ROM Encyclopedias," *Searcher*, vol. 6, no. 4, April 1998, p. 57.

21. This checklist is drawn from my own research and thoughts about CD-ROM design for information retrieval and from the evaluation checklists developed in Veronica Harry and Charles Oppenheim, "Evaluations of Electronic Databases, Part 1: Criteria for Testing CD-ROM Products." *Online and CD-ROM Review*, vol. 17, no. 4, 1993, pp. 211–22; Péter Jacsó, CD-ROM Software, Dataware, and Hardware: Evaluation, Selection, and Installation, Englewood, Colo.: Libraries Unlimited, 1992; McFaul, op. cit., pp. 18–29; Richards and Robinson, op. cit., pp. 96–101; and Jennifer Rowley and Frances Slack, "The Evaluation of Interface Design on CD-ROMS," *Online and CDRom Review*, vol. 21, no. 1, 1997, p. A44.

5 Web Sites: Weaving Deceit?

The World Wide Web is the *killer app* of the 1990s, turbo-charging a communications revolution that is redefining the information-seeking habits of Western civilization. What started off in 1969 at the height of the Cold War as an experimental network called ARPANET forms the backbone of the World Wide Web. A British scientist, Timothy Berners-Lee, is credited with devising the Web information architecture in 1989: a delivery system that relies on hypertext linking while harnessing the muscle-power of the Internet to string together countless and disparate computer databases.[1] With capabilities that zoom past CDs, the Web offers users a plethora of changing information resources, widespread access and delivery through telephone lines at next-to-nothing costs, multimedia, interactivity, and transactional and authoring capabilities.

Many libraries, educational institutions, and businesses have responded to the unflagging demand for Web access by crowding workstations into their settings and tackling the monumental task of providing one-on-one end-user training. But trainers are finding that the Web's learning curve is relatively steep, especially compared to those of CDs, video, or online catalogs, which are the Web's less-complex predecessors. One study about Web proficiency indicates that most beginners require at least five hours of

93

Design in a Nutshell

Few would dispute that the Web has potential to become the ultimate multimedia information delivery system. But for now, the Web is in its infancy, struggling to fulfill its unrealized promise. The Web remains an uncertainty—a diverse, creative, and volatile information space. Made up of millions of individual interfaces, the Web has design that directly counters many of the user-centered design tenets hammered out by the HCI community for conventional software development over the past twenty years.

Despite the Web's total design fluidity, users' tasks on the Web are becoming more specific. The Web is becoming an information source for users who are trying to solve problems. The shift from surfing to information retrieval eclipses the Web's earlier and highly anticipated role as an entertainment medium. Instead, users have focused on the Web as an information tool, collecting a small pool of addresses of sites that support their interests and that they return to with some regularity.

Interface design for information retrieval is different from design for surfing. In fact, the design for each genre has little overlap or compatibility. Users looking for information seek out sites that are concise, fast, and efficient, blocking out and ignoring irrelevant graphics and busy animation whenever possible. For information-seekers, the briefer the contact with the site, the more favorable the experience. Compared to their use of computer-based systems like CDs and software, users' behavior is different when they are looking for information on the Web. They scan Web sites for information; they do not read a page's text word-for-word. Also, users resist forming elaborate mental models about sites, which would give them a basis for figuring out how a site works and how it is structured. Users, because of their diversity, also have particular problems deciphering domain names and second-guessing where links might lead. Reference work on the Web is primitive at best, and users are far from being alike. Still, design tends to support generalized information retrieval tasks, like finding a known item.

The usability of the Web is hampered by the sheer lack of consistency in Web design. The free-for-all nature of the Web gives designers an inexpensive playground for creativity. The lack of design rules or standards, however, makes mastering Web prototypes difficult. Devices from traditional software for user forgiveness, especially prompts for saving work, are largely absent from Web applications. HCI researchers have begun arguing for usability on the Web, which is derived from their growing base of experimental usability testing. One of the biggest usability sore spots is navigation. While designers debate the merits of shell systems, a majority of users are oblivious to nuances of structure and prefer to "navigate in the moment" and work off a system that is based on remembering where they came from last.

Multimedia, once the darling of new media, has become an unnerving vexation for most information-seekers on the Web. Among a segment of designers, the use of graphics tends to be motivated by "eyeball-hustling," instead of value-adding to the context of the text, which information-seekers desire. As a result, a majority of users looking for information tend to ignore graphics altogether and stick to the text. With text comes a whole host of readability issues. Since users scan Web content, the hunt for information is enhanced when white space is artfully limited, horizontal rules are not used, and there are no more than five choices per screen. The writing style of Web content matters, too. Users better the time they spend on tasks and remember more of what they have read when content is short, concise, scannable, and written in a style that has more of an objective tone than a promotional one.

The Web has unlocked a world of information resources that were once unavailable to users with disabilities. Ironically, though, the majority of Web design has little awareness in its support of this user group's diverse set of needs and access limitations. Web design features, such as tables, columns, frames, and embedded links, regularly cause significant accessibility problems for users with special needs. Users with visual limitations, especially blindness, are regularly locked out of sites because the assistive technologies they use with computers, such as screen readers, translate pages literally from left to right and from top to bottom, jumbling the readings of tables and columns. Design guidelines for accessibility consistently advocate building flexibility into sites and providing alternative cues for functions.

solid hands-on instruction before they can use a browser and author a basic Web page in hypertext mark-up language (HTML).[2] Still, for a majority of users, no matter how much training they receive, the Web remains a chaotic mess; an exploratory abyss that is nothing more than a time bandit, trading in eclecticism and vastness. To combat usability problems, intermediaries from a range of disciplines have stepped in, armed with guidelines and recommendations for evaluating, selecting, and using Web sites that have reliable content as well as usable designs.

Design Analysis
Task Support: Stranger in a Strange Land

Task support is a conundrum on the Web. As we saw throughout part 1, task support, meeting users' expectations for fulfilling tasks, is the foundation of user-centered interface design. The traditional HCI approach to designing interfaces in the software industry is to assess end users' goals and to design within that context. But when it comes to the Web, many of these design tenets give way. From infrastructure to end users, the Web is a variable and volatile environment. If anything is widely acknowledged about Web design, it is that interface design on the Web is *not* the same as commercial software design. Ben Shneiderman describes the new world of the Web:

> The World Wide Web is an astonishing development which is producing radical societal changes in less than a decade. It is as revolutionary as printing, the telephone, and television all wrapped up in one throbbing monster. Pay attention to it. Ride it if you can, and watch out for the fire. There are twin thrills in the World Wide Web. First it allows many people to publish information, communicate, entertain, and provide services. Second it reaches a remarkably diverse set of users. However, there are triple threats in the World Wide Web: the users' environments are highly varied, quality control is shaky, and rugged independence limits common interface design patterns.[3]

The uniqueness of the Web has left many HCI researchers puzzled. Unlike software environments, the Web has no defined user base; no set of tasks that have a beginning, middle, and an end; and no control over system requirements. Many users behave differently on the Web, too, basing their preferences on content rather than on their success with accessing information, as they do when evaluating traditional software.[4] The many differences between the two media have left HCI researchers sorting out which findings from HCI about software design are applicable to Web design. A recent accounting of their findings appears in Table 5.1 (see page 98).[5]

Since the beginning, trying to categorize the Web in terms of users and their tasks has been problematic because of the medium's newness, immenseness, and transience. A large survey of Web users conducted in 1996

Table 5.1   *What Makes the Web Different from Software?*

Defining Characteristics of the Web

- Used by a variety of users

- Used on a variety of different platforms

- Rapid evolution

- Boundaries between interfaces are fuzzy

- Professionals and amateurs share the same space

- Variability among the types of sites

- Fluid boundaries of size and time

- Intangibility of the medium

- Runs on multiple servers

- Decentralization of development and maintenance

- Unknown entry points by users

- Variety of skills required does not match developer skills

- Lack of gate-keeping

- Presence of online advertising

- Competition for space with other sites

- Importance of first impressions

- Needs time to load

- Open versus closed community

- Page as a defined unit

- Browser as an intermediary

- Catering to minority interests

- Multipurpose sites

• Less clear stage of interface development

• No taxonomy

• Automatic usage logging

• Less private than software

Source:"Usability Testing of World Wide Web Sites,"SIGCHI WWW SIA: CHI 97, ACM Conference, http://www.acm.org/sigchi/web/ chi97testing/ricknote.htm, accessed 2/19/99.

found that 77 percent of 59,000 respondents vaguely described their primary activity on the Web as "browsing."[6] Still another perspective came years ago from a fellow researcher I know who aptly couched the emerging Web in strangely philosophical terms: "You just have to believe that there is no single place called the Web," he said. "You cannot touch it, or visit its headquarters, or call up its help line."[7] In general, Web sites are like contours of a diamond, endless facets reflecting light from within. On a fair number of sites, task support runs amok because user-centered design has been superseded by individualistic expression.

Nevertheless, the reasons behind how and why people use the Web are coming into view in two important ways. First, a majority of the Web's content increasingly falls into categories of purpose, the first inklings of order and methodology. A recent HCI paper breaks down sites into four categories that are information-based: *Informational sites* that supply information about organizations, their products or services; *search* sites that are made up of extensive databases; *transactional* sites that behave like products; and *multipurpose* portal sites that combine elements of each one of these categories.[8] Each one of these four types of sites defines the Web's purpose as information-based. Entertainment sites, which were once a highly anticipated destination of the Web, have fallen short of expectations because technological capabilities have lagged as much as five years behind the promise and hype.[9]

The second change (a by-product of the first) is that users are turning to the Web to carry out a set of tasks different from free-spirited exploration. Information retrieval has replaced random surfing.[10] A majority of users have come to view the Web as a source of information for solving problems. As a result, users are increasingly cubby-holing a coterie of sites on their browser bookmarks, sites that give them entree into information spaces that are usable and that support their interests. In fact, one study states that over half the pages that people access are revisits and only a few pages are accessed with any frequency.[11] More and more, users are making a conscious decision to shrink the aperture of the Web, exerting whatever control they have over the system.

Web design is at a strange crossroads; exploratory, laissez-faire panache is becoming superseded by eyeball-grabbing seriousness. A shift in Web use toward information retrieval underlies the evaluation of Web information resources, not only in terms of content (which is beyond the scope of this book), but also in terms of design. The first thing an evaluator should know is that Web design that supports information retrieval is different from design that enhances browsing. Some of the most extensive usability testing about information retrieval on the Web has been (and continues to be) conducted by Jared Spool and his colleagues at User Interface Engineering. (See "Pick of the Lot" recommended readings in Table 5.8 on page 129.) Their testing has found, for instance, that features that satisfy surfers, such as animation that is full of surprises and fun, tend to, in most cases, only frustrate and slow the hunt for information-seekers.[12] Sites that try to support both activities, surfing and information retrieval, tend to fizzle. In one study, subjects physically covered up animated elements on the screen so they could increase concentration on the task at hand.[13]

As this chapter's field test shows (see page 102), when it comes to information retrieval on the Web, users care about speed and efficient design that hastens decision making. The guidelines for Web design that were developed at Yale University provide a good summary of design basics to look for when evaluating information retrieval sites:

The best-designed reference Web sites allow users to quickly pop
into the site, find what they want, and then easily print or
download what they find. Typically, there is no "story" to tell, so
the usage patterns are totally non-linear. Content and menu
structure must be carefully organized to support fast search and
retrieval, easy downloading of files, and convenient printing
options . . . contact time is brief, the shorter, the better.[14]

A key component of Web design for information retrieval is conciseness. From
usability tests, a profile of how Web users look for information is emerging. In
particular, Web users scan sites for content, instead of reading the text word-for-
word.[15] Users also spend little time trying to figure out how a site is organized.[16]
As a time-saving strategy, about a third of users looking for information will try
a site's search engine.[17] Users typically encounter two problems with this so-called
strategy.[18] First, what is conveyed about a search interface may not provide users
with enough information about the scope of the collection that they are about to
search. Is the whole site being searched or just a narrow set of pages? Better yet, is
there any way to specify an area for searching and exclude other areas that are
totally irrelevant? When users are met with incomplete information, many will
spend time guessing what percentage of the site they are actually searching,
slowing the hunt. Second, once a search is carried out, users often have difficulty
interpreting their search results.[19] Haphazardly organized information,
redundant links, and incomplete headings all set back users since they must
venture through the links, trying to find a match to their original query.

One recent critic of the Web's potential for research work argued that
"search engines in general, with their half-baked algorithms, are closer to slot
machines than library catalogues."[20] In many cases, users must do more work
than the interface ever delivers in return. Frustration levels and cognitive
overload, a pair of recurring problems on the Web, are likely to increase. Not
surprisingly, Web users in institutional settings, like schools, prefer having

Field Test:
Southwest Airlines Ticketing Web Site

(http://iflyswa.com)

The holiday was rapidly approaching and time was running out. I had procrastinated about making my airline reservations for a trip home to see my family. Late one night, when the local travel agency that I usually go to was long closed, I decided to make my travel plans with an airline Web site. All the ads had tried to convince me how easy the sites were to use. Still, I was skeptical. When it came to my computer and the Web, nothing was easy.

After a quick load, a virtual reservation desk for Southwest Airlines appeared on the screen. On the opening page below the banner touting "Double Rewards" was an image of a phone labeled "Reservations" and a large red arrow saying "Try Me" that pointed to the phone. What I needed to get done, make a reservation, was right out in front. I was on my way. The page was laid out simply and clearly, the headings made obvious sense and there were not many of them, leaving me far from feeling overwhelmed with useless information and graphics. At last, I was in command of the Web! My mouse was drawn to the phone before I knew what happened.

The ticketing information screen quickly popped up with large lettering, showing a link to a map of cities that Southwest Airlines serves. I ignored the map and went with the scrolling tables of cities listed in alphabetical order, showing departure, arrival, and return times. Selection was quick and easy, I had a choice, and I did not have to rely on my geography skills and the map. My sense of accomplishment drew me to scroll farther down the page to the next table labeled "Approximate Travel Times." Four small pictures of three happy suns and one moon indicated different time periods so clearly that I barely glanced at the lettering beneath the images that stated "before 10 AM," "10 AM–2 PM," "2 PM–6 PM," and "after 6 PM." Clicking the standard Web form selection bullet was again intuitive, and I did not hesitate to try the "Dates for Departures" and "Arrivals" table. Before I knew what happened, I had selected the days and months from the scrolled tables.

Even so, I hesitated over the button labeled "Show Schedule." Everything was so easy, my skepticism returned. Surely something would go awry. I gathered my courage and clicked the button. The second screen popped up quickly and gave me another table, showing departure and arrival times for the dates I had selected. I could change the date by clicking arrows pointing to the right or left at the top of the table. Alternative price information was displayed in separate columns. Information about the pricing was available by clicking on the column header, which was a link to an explanation of that price option (time limits, refunds, etc.) I selected time and price alternatives by clicking the Web form selection bullet. Afterward, I continued to the next screens that handled billing. At the bottom of each screen, I had the option of stopping my ticketing. This let me feel in control of what I was doing. Also, I could scroll through the screen before I entered anything to see what potential land mines or unexpected traps lay ahead.

Overall, I was pleased with what I had accomplished with ease and speed. When the schedule for my search was displayed, I had the flexibility to change my dates of travel or I could start over again. This was a time-saver, because I did not have to back out of the program each time I wanted to revise my search. There was also more forgiveness worked into the design. I noticed that, when I made a mistake, a friendly graphic appeared and offered straightforward directions about what was wrong with what I was doing. If I clicked on the Help button, it gave directions that applied to what I was doing then. In interface design, this kind of feature is known as *context-sensitive* help because assistance is directly provided about what is happening on the screen. Context-sensitive help, a rarity on the Web, saved me time and kept me focused on my task.

When I finished booking the flight, I did not feel as though I had wrestled with travel schedules and impossible search criteria. Everything was selected from tables and entered into Web forms. Even with my limited online shopping experience, I found the forms intuitive, with a lot of transferability from things I already knew. It was as if I were marking up a printed schedule to show my travel agent. What gave me the greatest feeling of comfort was that I could stop the ticketing right until the very end. The colors and graphics were simple so they loaded quickly. Moreover, this is an occasion where a GUI worked, adding understanding to the selection process because buttons were large, clearly labeled, and consistent from screen to screen.

The iflyswa.com site was truly easy to use for information retrieval and transactions. It was intuitive, especially regarding navigation, and enhanced by graphics and consistent color coding. The end result: Making choices was flexible and less stressful than dealing with travel agents. I had time to make up my mind about what I wanted. I felt in control of my flight plans and the interface I was using to make them. It was fun. In fact, I wanted to book another flight, but I had no place to go. I started to imagine where I could go, and rather than just closing the browser, I went back to the opening screen and poked around with my mouse. I did not have to worry about a long line of impatient people behind me.

Field testing of iflyswa.com was performed and written up the week of August 24–August 28, 1998, by Enid Irwin, San Jose State University Graduate School of Library and Information Science and Hewlett-Packard Company.

a hands-on trainer nearby to head off the time-consuming vexations of the Web.

Even if these design pitfalls are avoided, the activity of reference work has definite limitations on the Web. In the pre-Web world, librarians instilled users with organizational schemes, such as LC (Library of Congress) subject headings that have the ability to unlock access to most of the knowledge contained in Western civilization. Now, with the Web, users are required to crack the classification scheme of every interface they encounter—on their own. As Lou Rosenfeld (who is interviewed at the end of this chapter) points out, most sites used for information retrieval do not support the complete range of how users actually look for information. In his book, *Information Architecture for the World Wide Web*, Rosenfeld and his co-author, Peter Morville, present a continuum of information-seeking behavior that information sites on the Web should support but rarely do. In general, users can be either looking for a known item, searching for something that cannot be fully described, exploring or browsing, or conducting comprehensive research.[21] An information-seeker can wear any and all of these hats at any given time. Information retrieval interfaces on the Web need to take this into account.

In light of these thoughts, it is not surprising that the vast and diverse user base of the Web has had considerable difficulties ferreting out what means what on the Web. One particular problem occurs for users when they need to decipher the meaning of domain and link names, which are often composed with jargon or abstraction or both.[22] Before its redesign, Travelocity.com contained an example of this design flaw. The popular travel site, created by Sabre travel reservation systems, stumped many users by using jargon for a heading for what the industry calls "trip segments" but what most users call round-trip or one-way.[23] In general, the level of knowledge that the diverse user base may possess can hinder basic information retrieval tasks. A usability study at Microsoft showed that a certain part of the population lacked the necessary skills for locating a site from an image map—15 percent of their subjects thought that Madagascar was in Europe.[24] Users also have great difficulties when they need to compare two facts found on separate sites.[25] During testing conducted by User Interface Engineering, the only way that they could complete the task was to remember the fact, physically write it down on paper, or print it out from their printer. In this case, the browser (Netscape)—an intermediary interface for navigating the Web—hindered the information retrieval process. The difficulty users experienced with the task colored their perception of the site, which they considered incomplete and inferior.[26] Finally, the functionality of Web applications works against what reference work needs most, the ability to retain information. Prompts that give users the option to save their work are absent in most, if not all, Web applications.[27] Consequently, users may click an interesting link, wander out of an application to a new destination, and lose their work all at the same time.

Usability: Lessons Unlearned?

Web design guidelines, blueprints for consistency and usability, are as diverse and contradictory as recipes for meat loaf. One study of 21 sites offering Web design guidelines found 357 unique recommendations for "good design."[28] The two most frequently cited recommendations among the lot were for a signature at the bottom of the page and for "Here" not to be used to designate a link. Not only are these and many other recommendations prescriptively confined, many design guides are drawn from personal preferences, instead of sounder methods of experimentation and usability testing.[29] Nevertheless, there are some emerging signs of uniformity on the Web, which give users an incipient design language for understanding it. Underlined text, for example, has become nearly ubiquitous for signifying hypertext links. Still, though, the amount of text that is underlined varies and this can significantly impact a site's usability. Users have better luck with text links that are phrases (instead of single words) and that can be clearly picked out instead of embedded in a block of dense text.[30]

For the most part, Web design is still about creativity and diversity instead of usability and conformity. Besides the sheer vastness of Web design, a barrier to consistency has been partially caused by dominating Web styles that are constantly in flux. Jakob Nielsen has chronicled Web styles since 1993 and his commentary appears in Table 5.2 on the next page.[31]

Nielsen has argued that Web design has yet again morphed. The new design paradigm concerns managing and organizing Web sites so that design templates with more usability are enforced.[32] David Siegel, the Web design guru and author of the best-selling *Creating Killer Web Sites*, has similarly argued that Web design projects need to be as formalized as architecture.[33] Many organizations are just beginning to recognize the need for usability in their own Web and intranet sites, especially as the Web becomes more competitive and the monetary benefits for usable sites are calculated. Sun Microsystems is a prime example. A user survey at Sun showed that employees typically use about 12 of the company intranet pages each day and two new sub-sites a week.[34] Nielsen, who headed up the redesign of Sun's intranet interface and instituted company-wide design and navigation standards, figures that the reworked site now saves employees about five minutes per week and delivers a savings of as much as $10 million annually back into the company's coffers in increased productivity.[35]

Other Web developers, too, have argued that usability testing, findings, and standards will underwrite the success of individual Web sites in the near future. According to the Yale Web Guidelines, the Web and institutional intranets "are no longer just a playground for local 'gearheads.' Patchy, heterogeneous design standards and a lack of cohesive central planning can cripple any attempt to realize productivity gains through an intranet."[36] Designing for usability on the Web is tricky, though, since usability problems occur in differing proportions on the Web than they do with traditional

Table 5.2   A History of Web Site Styles According to Jakob Nielsen

1993   Just having a server on the Web was enough to show you were a pioneer! I remember faithfully going to "What's New with NCSA Mosaic" every day to see who was putting stuff up on the Web. The pages may have sucked like a vacuum, but they came to us from the other side of the world, which caused a novelty effect.

1994   The main thing in 1994 was to show users how much information you had. This was the year of home pages that were no more than glorified hot lists with long bulleted lists of links. At this relatively early stage on the Web, people were easily impressed by anybody who had real, useful content.

1995   Focused, value-added information became key as users suffered under ever-increasing information overload. The preferred style for home page design in 1995 was to provide a clear sense of priority for the user and to showcase a small amount of high-quality information. "Less is more" definitely became a key design strategy.

1996   I think that Web surfing is dead. Sure, users may check out a few new sites every now and then, just as they may buy a new magazine from the newsstand when they are stranded in O'Hare. But to continue the magazine analogy, most users will probably spend the majority of time with a small number of Web sites that meet their requirements with respect to quality and content.

1997   We will finally see real community on the Web. The term "community" is much misused among Internet pundits, and most current Web sites have less community than a city bus—at least all the passengers are going in the same direction. We need Web sites that truly allow users with common interests to provide value-added services for each other. Also, real business will happen on the Web (that is, sites will have to do something real for customers and not just be online brochures).

Source: Jakob Nielsen, "User Interface Design for the WWW," CHI 97 Proceedings, http://www.acm.org/sigchi/chi97/proceedings/tutorial/jn.html, accessed 2/19/99.

Table 5.3   Usability Problems on the Web

• Unclear labeling and vocabulary

• Users need to remember too much

• Graphics are cluttered and overused

• Inaccurate understanding of site design

• Poor match between site design and users' needs

• Navigation problems

• Designed without clear target-user populations in mind

• Design is not guided by users' goals

• Insufficient privacy and security

• Inadequate buy-in from stakeholders

Source: "Usability Testing of World Wide Web Sites," SIGCHI WWW SIA: CHI 97, ACM Conference, http://www.acm.org/sigchi/web/chi97 testing/ricknote.htm, accessed 2/19/99.

software. A list of Web usability issues from a brainstorming session at the '97 HCI conference appears in Table 5.3.[37]

Not surprisingly, navigation is one of the biggest sources of usability problems on the Web. Navigational hypertext systems, in general, are rife with design trade-offs. Not only do users need to find information efficiently, they also need to find their way back from where they came, find all of the relevant information on the site that they need for task support, and still have freedom to explore.[38] In one study, over a third of Web users have reported trouble locating pages and another third have trouble organizing retrieved information.[39] Part of this problem is associated with Web design itself, which makes little use of navigational landmarks that could communicate to users where they are and where they can go. For users, landmarks—navigational bars, logos, and headers—are the difference between a clearly marked footbridge and a raging river they will have to ford.

The wide variability of design, the constant change, and the sheer number of Web sites (four million and counting) has created an environment that the majority of users prefer to "navigate in the moment."[40,41] Most users navigate the Web by remembering where they came from before, a limited approach that quickly taxes users' short-term memory capabilities.[42] By using this technique, users avoid developing mental models about individual Web sites, a practice they more readily apply when using software as they try to figure out how a site might be structured and work.[43] As a result, the actual structuring of sites may, on one level, have less impact on users who resist second-guessing or fully learning a site's structure, which is subject to change anyhow.[44] Even in Sun's Web style guide, the authors advise against using a palette of graphic navigation buttons:

> Most people will not be spending enough time looking at your pages to learn the meaning of the buttons. In addition, people will be creating links to your pages from other pages with dissimilar navigation landmarks. Icon palettes work in large, widely used, closed systems, and are often combined with other, textual navigation hints.[45]

Navigational devices, which could potentially help users determine how to use a site, tend to be underused by users.[46] One explanation is that users need to first understand the overall purpose and context of a site before they can cognitively fill in the pieces of how features like tables and frames fit.[47] The need that users have for context may be why a majority of users turn to site maps. Site maps can provide an overall context, not just a scrollable piece, of the site or the page. Like a print preview command in a software package, Web devices that give users a complete visual overview of options are prized. Navigational bars at the bottom and top of pages are another example of devices that ease navigating. Bars are especially easy to absorb when they have fewer than seven key functions.[48]

A whole other issue with Web design is how interactivity is used. Although Web pundits sing the praises of the medium's interactivity, the truth is that its joys are more often associated with financial transactions than with informational ones. When the *Wall Street Journal* sent two dozen major corporate Web sites an e-mail question, the response was dismal.[49] Of the sample, nine sites never responded, two took three weeks to reply, and the rest sent form responses that were off-topic. Only three Web sites provided a relevant response within a day. Similarly, when an investor services group tried to gauge how long it took to get an e-mail response from a site, they found 30 percent of customer messages never got a response.[50]

Aesthetics: But Is It Art?

A well-executed use of color, images, and typography can sharpen users' perceptive abilities like a double shot of espresso in the morning. Aesthetics can either make or break any information-based interface, delivering a whole other dimension to users that eases navigation and usability. Yet, when it comes to Web design, and particularly sites for information retrieval, aesthetics take the prize as the medium's most talked-about and highly anticipated . . . letdown. Yes, letdown. One author, discussing graphic development on the Web, writes:

> Rather than being seen as a solution to some of the Web's usability problems, graphic design is often regarded as their source. Graphics are seen as extraneous, bandwidth-hogging nuisances to users (which, unfortunately, they often are). Designers are viewed as mean-spirited prima donnas concerned only with churning out useless visual distractions that glitter and sparkle on the screen.[51]

Part of the problem with Web graphics is that they usually are not geared toward helping users get their work done. In information-based sites, clear and consistent icons, graphical identity schemes, and graphical overviews can do wonders in helping users find what they came for, without wasting too much of their time.[52] Instead, many Web designers are motivated by attention-grabbing; the more interesting the site is, the more time users will spend on it. Another part of the problem when graphics are used to present information is what Sun's Web style guide describes as a vexing trade-off for developers, where there is "tension between the amount of 'packaging' that you do to your content and your audience's desire to get information they need as efficiently as possible."[53] Still another problem occurs with porting the print medium over to the Web, where the medium's opportunities and users' behavior differs. For all of these reasons and more, graphic design on the Web, so far, does little to impact how users find information.[54] In fact, most users ignore graphics and seek out textual links for navigation instead.[55]

Not long ago, the breaking point in user patience with conventional software interfaces was measured in minutes. Now, the breaking point in user patience on the Web is figured to be about 10 seconds.[56] In most cases, multimedia on the Web—full-scale images, sound, and animation—are guaranteed time-wasters that frustrate users. The slowness of the downloads, the irrelevance of the image to the site's content, and the distraction caused by garish design all work against users' turning to the Web for information retrieval. For example, one user looking for the lowest-priced flight to London in a usability test completely missed finding the answer because the information was contained in an animated ad at which he refused to ever look.[57] Video is hardly any different. One of the biggest problems cited about video is that it tends to feature "talking heads," which add little or no value to moving away from the purely textual medium.[58]

Despite the information-seekers' generalizable discontent with visuals on the Web, there are emerging ground rules for effectively using graphics. A section of Sun's Web style guide, reprinted in Table 5.4 (see page 114), offers guidelines for designers but has great applicability for evaluators, too, who are judging how graphics are used on existing sites.[59]

So far, one of the most pressing aesthetic issues in information retrieval on the Web deals with the readability of text. Early human factors studies have reported that users read online documents anywhere from 20 percent to 30 percent more slowly from a computer screen than from a print copy.[60] Even with screen resolution improvements that have occurred since these studies were first carried out, reading is an activity that is still decidedly slower online. There is also another issue. On the Web, reading is an entirely different activity. Users skim and scan Web sites when they are looking for information, instead of reading the site's content word-for-word.[61,62]

Sites that facilitate scanning have a simplified *virtual landscape* so that spatial information can be easily absorbed and retained.[63] In particular, Web usability findings suggest that pages should not be overloaded with choices. One guideline suggests that no more than seven choices per page should be used, unless the information is grouped as a chunk.[64] White space is another component affecting scanabilitiy; it should be used sparingly because it "spreads out information and slows the hunt."[65] Light background colors cause the text on the page to stand out and make it is easier to read.[66] In one case, readability of Web pages was notched up by as much as 124 percent when Nielsen and his crew at Sun rewrote the content of a site in a more Web-friendly style, so that the text was shorter (by half), scannable, and more objective than promotional.[67] The rewritten version bettered users' task times by 80 percent, reduced their task error rates by 809 percent, increased memory by 100 percent, and satisfaction levels by 37 percent.[68]

Web Design for Users with Special Needs

People with disabilities constitute a significant percentage of the population that will only continue to increase as people live longer lives.

Table 5.4 Sun's Guide for Web Graphics

• Use graphics critical to the information content of your page.

• Limit large images used solely for visual appeal.

• Keep the total size of all images used on a page to less than 30K.

• Use available technology tricks to minimize content access time.

• Avoid message-critical JPEG images if you want the largest audience possible.

• Warn the audience if a link leads to a large graphic.

• Minimize the number of colors used in a single image.

• If you're going to use many images close together on a page, consider how quickly the images will load as a group due to the variability among users' browsers and bandwidths.

• Include alternative text for each image.

• Use images with transparent backgrounds to better integrate your images.

• Don't use graphics referenced from another site.

• Use graphical bullets for a purpose, not because they look "neat."

• Use graphical divider bars sparingly.

• Use a small set of bullets or accent graphics consistently, if they are used at all.

• Take care with background images.

• Explicitly setting the text color on a Web page comes with some interesting human costs (e.g., color-blind users may not be able to read the page).

• Preview your images on several hardware and browser combinations.

Source: Sun's Guide to Web Style (http://www.sun.com/styleguide/tables/Navigation.html) accessed 2/19/99.

Here are some of the commonly cited figures. More than 43 million Americans have a disability of some type.[69] About 15 percent of the population has a disability that is "severe enough to interfere with work or otherwise constitute a serious handicap."[70] As the population continues to age, the likelihood of developing a disability increases 25 percent by age 55 and jumps to 50 percent by age 65.[71] In fact, it is a fair assessment to assume that all individuals have a range of capabilities that fluctuates due to age, task, environment, or injury, which may cause them to be less abled at different times in their lives.[72] For members of the disabled community, the Web is a mixed blessing. On one hand, the Web is a savior, offering many users with disabilities first-time access to a large number of information resources for which they have long hungered. On the other hand, the Web is a demon, plaguing users with special needs, who pay dearly for Web access in time and patience. Unfortunately, most Web design is oblivious to users with disabilities and their needs, their limitations, and even their actual use of the Web for research work.

When it comes to computers, there are no typical, unencumbered users. One author has even argued that "from the point of view of a computer, *all* human users are handicapped."[73] In general, DOS, UNIX, and LYNX text-based environments have given many computer users with disabilities, especially users that are visually impaired or blind, command interface styles they could eventually master, especially with the help of some assistive technologies (e.g., a screen reader or a screen magnifier). But with the sweeping adoption of windowing and graphical interfaces, which are dependent on pointing, clicking, and seeing, users with visual disabilities and/or physical limitations have experienced great difficulty adapting. Surprisingly, members of the HCI community, who are strong advocates of user-centered design, have played a relatively small role in developing systems that could accommodate users with disabilities. Some authors have argued that the neglect is spurred by economics: The high costs of designing for users with disabilities far outweigh the monetary benefits of serving such a small market.[74] Others admit that "users with disabilities are clearly not on the radar screen of mainstream HCI."[75] Traditionally, accessibility has been defined in a broad context, dealing with removing barriers that prevent people with disabilities from participating in life's activities.[76] But accessibility is a primary dimension of HCI, too, especially as the concept relates to task support and usability. If a blind user pulls up a Web page to discover tomorrow's weather forecast but cannot see the image map—even with the aid of a screen reader that cannot register the presence of any image—then the interface clearly does not support the user's research task and is far from being accessible.

As a general rule of thumb, poorly designed Web pages are hard to use whether the user is disabled or not. But the difference is that, depending on the nature of a user's disability, a poorly designed Web page can present far more significant, if not insurmountable, barriers to users with special needs than to those without. Adding to access problems are the varying consequences bad design has for users with different types and degrees of disabilities.[77] At best, the interaction effects between users with disabilities and Web use are only generalizable.[78]

Users that are visually impaired, for example, experience instantaneous overload with Web sites that have a variety of fonts, colors, and layouts, especially when they are using a screen magnifier that allows them to only view individual segments of a screen, one small section at a time. Users that are blind have severe trouble with sites that have convoluted ordering schemes and too many choices per screen. Much of their interaction is dependent on deciphering and memorizing what a screen reader reads back to them as it automatically reads each page, regardless of frames and tables, from left to right. Users with hearing impairments may not be able

Field Test:
CNN Interactive News Web Site

(http://www.cnn.com)

What frustrates you about the Web? Slow-loading screens? Cluttered, disorganized pages? Too many links to make sense of? OK. Now, imagine you're blind. The page source, with none of the graphics and headlines that help organize the visible page, is being read aloud to you in monotone by a very literal speech-synthesizer called a *screen reader*. You have to listen and to remember the relative position in sequence of anything you might want to review or any link you may want to follow, making a mental outline of the page as you hear it. If the page uses audio, it is inaccessible to you because the screen reader is already making use of your computer's sound card. Click on a link that takes you to an entirely different site? Good luck finding your way back. If you do get back, your friendly screen reader will insist on re-reading the whole page (including the ads) until you reach the point from which you linked out. No, don't try to imagine it. If you are sighted, you can't even begin. And have we mentioned hearing disabilities, or mobility impairments that make using a mouse or keyboard or both impossible? Now combine a few of these, because many people have multiple disabilities, and they commingle and complicate users' interactions even further.

As field testers, we recognized early on that it would be impossible for us as temporarily "abled" users to run an objective product test for users with disabilities. At a minimum, we needed access to the assistive technologies that open the Web to people with disabilities. We were fortunate to work with Eric Christierson, Adaptive Computer Specialist at San Jose State University's Disabled Resource Center (http://www.drc.sjsu.

edu), who is legally blind and with minimal vision at a nose-to-the-screen range. Eric regularly trains students with visual disabilities on how to use the Web for research. He agreed to show us around the CNN news site. Eric uses the Jaws screen reader from Henter-Joyce, Inc. (http://www.hj.com) in a Windows 98 environment with Microsoft Internet Explorer. As he points out, this means that there are three interacting sets of commands occurring at the same time. Some browsers work better with assistive technology than others: The current Internet Explorer has built-in compatibilities with the newest version of Jaws for Windows, released in July of 1998, which he considers a good first step. (For the following exploration, the Jaws commands were set to be on top wherever possible.)

As the opening screen loads, Eric says, "CNN is a page I usually avoid. There's too much going on with the design." That is true even for a sighted user: Javascript banners, image map, left-margin table of contents, and two columns of content, including 15 links. For abled users, HCI findings show that our ability to process information begins to fail at about seven items. This screen gives us twice that many. Another consideration: Most Web surfers will not scroll down more than two screens. CNN's main page is five screens deep. Lengthy as this is for us, it's interminable when read aloud— even at the 300 words per minute an experienced user like Eric can comprehend. "It takes as long as it takes," he says. "For most, it doesn't matter how long it takes, because there's no alternative. It's still better than not having access to this much information in a form that you have some control over."

Tabbing forward from link to link is faster, but still tedious. There is a faster way. Looking for something as specific as "Mark McGwire +homerun," we can use the search box, once we find it. CNN's is at the bottom of the page, and since Eric remembers this he can use the Page Down key till it hits bottom. Placing it at the top would be a friendlier design. But burying it in the middle of the page would be the worst design choice, frustrating non-sighted users even more. Generally, standardization on the Web is minimal and uniform search boxes are no exception. Some accept the "enter" key as a trigger, others require a mouse click, and few tell you which they require. Two HCI principles would have helped the design here: (1) Offer a choice of ways to use the feature; and (2) if one of them is a button, make that target big enough to hit easily. The keywords from our search are found in a paragraph on screen two and may be a link, but we cannot click on the link from here. Instead, the program takes us back to the start of the first page, and we must again pass through and read all of the content (including the ads) to reach the desired link.

The interface between Jaws for Windows and Internet Explorer has a feature that makes this whole process much easier. With a toggle, it reformats the page, (ignoring the images, which are useless here), extracts all the links and arranges them in alphabetical order. The links are easier to reach, easier to bypass (with the Page Down key), easier to click on accurately (since each one is a separate line at the left margin), and easier to remember because of the alphabetical structure. Of course, links that say merely "Click HERE!" are useless, but usability researchers have found that even sighted users navigate better with links that briefly and clearly describe the destination. However, not all pages can be reformatted in this way. Most screen readers cannot handle frames. They don't read what you would see on the screen, only the underlying HTML, and that may consist only of the word <FRAMESET> and a line of code. They have no way of moving from one frame into another. This means that the common practice of using one frame as a table of contents and giving no other navigation leaves screen readers literally clueless.

"I wondered if there was an image map here?" Eric asks. "Jaws doesn't pick it up at all." True enough. In the reformatted page, there is a link called "image map," but clicking on it invokes this message: Image map error: your client did not send any coordinates. Either your client does not support the image map or the map file was not accessed as a map. Remember, reformatting ignores images and the image map was not perceived by the screen reader at all when it read the page's underlying code.

We asked Eric what he considers the three worst usability problems on Web sites, in general. Frames and image maps are clearly the top two, but the third is a surprise: differences in font size. "Some screen readers will read straight across the page," he explains, "but when the text is in columns with different font sizes, the reader has difficulty telling which words are on the same line."

Field testing of cnn.com was performed by Eric Christierson, Adaptive Computer Specialist at San Jose State University's Disabled Resource Center, the week of September 8–September 12, 1998, observed by Alison Head and Jo Falcon, and written by Jo Falcon, San Jose State University Graduate School of Library and Information Science.

to hear audio and are unaware it even exists, unless a site provides closed-captioning too. Users with physical and mobility disabilities experience problems when navigation is dependent on pointing to a sequence of undersized buttons that are hard to physically isolate and to click. Each one of these brief examples narrowly addresses a few of the problems that occur among users with some disabilities.[79] Each Web experience for a user with a disability is bound to vary. To help fill out the picture, the field test described in the sidebar (on pages 117–120) provides a first-hand example of what it is actually like for a blind user to access the cnn.com news site.

As the field test illustrates, the Web can be a time-consuming labyrinth for users with disabilities, full of dead ends, false starts, and impassable barriers that quickly lead to cognitive overload and frustration. The HCI basics—task support, usability, and aesthetics—used throughout the book as a rubric for evaluating good design, are scarcely applicable in the world of Web users with disabilities. For evaluators trying to assess Web accessibility for users with special needs, a starting point is judging whether the site is universally designed or not. Among disabled-community advocates, there has been for some time a broad call for developers, manufacturers, and builders—of any products—to apply the principles of universal design.[80] Universal design accommodates the broadest range of users, regardless of their age or disability, by using consistently applied design basics and having built-in interface flexibility, allowing users with special needs to customize interfaces to match the full range of their particular needs. Indentations in sidewalks known as "curb cuts," which allow for wheelchair access (and even baby stroller access), are a well-acknowledged example of a universally designed product. Table 5.5 states the seven principles of universal design.[81]

The idea of universal design is relevant to how computers and information systems are developed and designed. Universal design advocates

---

Table 5.5 Universal Design Principles

Equitable use: Equitable use means that the design is useful and marketable to any group of users. To this end, it should:

- Provide the same means of use for all users: identical whenever possible, equivalent when not.

- Avoid segregating and stigmatizing any users.

- Provisions for privacy, security, and safety should be equally available to all users.

Flexibility in use: Flexibility in use means that the design accommodates a wide range of individual preferences and abilities. To achieve this goal, it should:

- Provide choice in methods and use.

- Accommodate right- or left-handed access and use.

- Facilitate the user's accuracy and precision.

- Provide adaptability to the user's pace.

Simple and intuitive use: Use of the design is easy to understand, regardless of the user's experience, knowledge, language skills, or current concentration level. It should:

- Eliminate unnecessary complexity.

- Be consistent with user expectations and intuition.

- Accommodate a wide range of literacy and language skills.

- Arrange information consistent with its importance.

- Provide effective prompting for sequential actions.

- Provide timely feedback during and after task completion.

Perceptible information: The design communicates necessary information effectively to the user regardless of ambient conditions or the user's sensory abilities. For this purpose, it should:

- Use different modes (pictorial, verbal, tactile) for redundant presentation of essential information.

- Provide adequate contrast between essential information and its surroundings.

- Maximize "legibility" of essential information and its surroundings.

- Differentiate elements in ways that can be described (i.e., make it easy to give instructions and directions).

- Provide compatibility with a variety of techniques or devices used by people with sensory limitations.

Tolerance of error: The design minimizes hazards and the adverse consequences of accidental or unintended actions. This principle requires that designers:

- Arrange elements to minimize hazards and errors: most used elements, most accessible, hazardous elements eliminated, isolated, or shielded.

- Provide warnings of hazards and errors.

- Provide fail-safe features.

- Discourage unconscious action in tasks that require vigilance.

Low physical effort: The design can be used efficiently and comfortably and with a minimum of fatigue. It should:

- Allow the user to maintain a neutral body position.

- Use reasonable operating forces.

- Minimize repetitive actions.

- Minimize sustained physical effort.

Size and space: Size and space for approach, reach, manipulation, and use are appropriate regardless of the user's body size, posture, or mobility. To this end, the design should:

- Provide a clear line of sight to important elements for any seated or standing user.

- Make reaching to all components comfortable for any seated or standing user.

- Accommodate variations in hand and grip size.

- Provide adequate space for the use of assistive devices or personal assistance.

Source: Eric Christierson and Donna Pantou, "Universal Design for Library Pages: Providing Access for Users with Disabilities," San Jose State University Faculty Diversity grant project, 1998.

have argued that the current definition of the average user is exclusionary, a fictitious construct that needs to be more realistically broadened to include users of all kinds and capabilities.[82] In particular, universally designed computer products should be accessible right out of the box, or be made accessible with the help of assistive technologies.[83] However, creating a mainstream awareness and practice of universal design principles— especially among a plethora of Web designers let loose with a creative new medium—has, so far, been a relatively slow and difficult process, even since the enactment of The Americans With Disabilities Act in 1990.[84,85] One author writes, "While universal design has been around for years, it is just beginning to gain acceptance in the mainstream computer community."[86]

Universal design principles are intentionally broad and take some extrapolation and interpretation to apply to the Web, but they are useful in clarifying issues of accessibility. Equally useful are specific Web guidelines, developed for creating sites that are accessible by users with disabilities. A compilation of accessible Web design principles appears in Table 5.6.[87]

Another valuable tool is Bobby, a free Web-based program developed by the Center for Applied Special Technology (CAST). Bobby quickly checks a

---

Table 5.6 Web Sites for Users with Disabilities Design Evaluation Checklist

• Individual pages of a site have a consistent and simple layout so that users with visual impairments or blind users using screen readers can more quickly navigate through a page and find the information they are trying to locate.

• Important information is placed at the top of the page since screen readers, commonly used by blind Web users, read from left to right, top to bottom.

• Alternative versions of pages exist, especially a text-only page that translates graphic and text information into one text-only page.

• Backgrounds should be kept simple with enough contrast so that users with low vision, color blindness, or black and white monitors can read the visual clues.

- Buttons are large and easy targets so that users with physical and mobile disabilities can select them easily from the screen.

- Functional features—buttons, scroll bars, and navigational bars—are identified as working functions instead of images.

- A site does not use hard coding: Application colors, graphical attributes, volume, font sizes, and styles can be adjusted by the user based on individual needs. When a font adjustment is made by a user, the page layout automatically resizes to match.

- Blinking or constantly changing text elements are not used, so that users with visual impairments, learning disabilities, or recurring headaches are not challenged. (Blinking tags have also been known to crash screen readers.)

- All images have descriptive alternative text (ALT tags) and, if possible, captions so that users who are visually impaired or blind and are using a screen reader know what exists on a page.

- Image maps include menu alternatives so that users who are visually impaired or blind can access embedded links.

- Video and audio segments include closed-captions so that users with hearing impairments and those who are using a screen reader (which may monopolize the system's sound card) have alternative methods for accessing the information. The page informs users that closed-captioning is available and includes instructions for use.

- Links have fully descriptive headings so that users using screen readers get the full context of the link's meaning. Sites that use "click here" are of little use because they do not impart any information for decision making.

- Tables, frames, and columns are used very sparingly, if at all, since the majority of screen readers that read from left to right will not distinguish separate cells of information in the translation.

- Plug-ins and Java applets should be used very sparingly, if at all. (Adobe Acrobat, in many cases, is not accessible with assistive technologies, even though Adobe is trying to rectify the problem.)

- A dividing character between links that occur consecutively is used so that a screen reader can distinguish between different links. Ideally, links are separated by more than just a new line.

- Sentences, headers, and list items end with punctuation so that screen readers can signal the shift to the user. (Screen readers do not recognize bullets or physical separation.)

- Pages include forms that can be downloaded and mailed or e-mailed later in case the user needs unavailable hands-on assistance with filling out the form.

site line by line and then issues a report that analyzes its accessibility for people with disabilities.[88] The Bobby seal of approval is a recognized symbol of a fully accessible site among Web users with disabilities. Not only is Bobby a powerful tool for designers, the program helps evaluators determine whether a Web site is accessible for users with special needs or not, and what is wrong with the underlying HTML that is used to format the page.

The Point

After Gutenberg printed the 42-line Bible in the mid-1400s, it took another 100 years for the book to become standardized; complete with an index, table of contents, and title pages.[89] Not surprisingly, the Web has a long way to go, too—if it's not usurped by the dazzle of another new medium in the meantime. For most users who now turn to the Web to carry out research, the medium is a lot like a frontier town, an outback for the self-reliant and tenacious. No matter what, the Web is packed with a choice of individual interfaces that are only a click away. If users become frustrated with the usability of one site, they are likely to move on to another. Help systems—a standardized fixture, however questionable, in most online products—are nearly nonexistent on Web sites.

Several years before the Web came into being, information design guru Edward Tufte introduced a faithful following of readers to visual strategies for taking users beyond the "flatland" of the page or the terminal screen. His approach emphasized working at "the intersection of image, word, number, and art, adding an invaluable dimension that conveys more meaning."[91] Similarly, when it comes to information retrieval on the Web, design founded at the intersection of emerging multimedia and how people actually look for information will turn out to be a driving force for taking Web users beyond the flatland. When Web design adapts more of a mutual goal of communicating purpose, audience, and tasks, only then will it become the mega-information resource that information-seekers increasingly expect. But for this transformation to occur, Web designers need to learn a lot more about visual and information design. A compilation of Web design evaluation criteria appears in Table 5.7.[90]

Table 5.7 Web Site Design Evaluation Checklist

- Purpose—what the site is about and the kind of information it has—and audience—who the site is intended for—are visibly identified and clearly described on the opening pages so that users know if the site will support their tasks or not.

- Useful content is pushed toward the top of the site and is easy to locate so that users' processing time is decreased.

- Site maps and/or tables of contents that provide users with an overall, visual schema of the site's contents are available, giving users insight into the site's organization and context.

- Users have a choice of search interfaces that support simple and advanced search modes so that interfaces have flexibility to support first-time and repeat users.

- Examples of search techniques and strategies, including the use of Boolean operators, are available so that users can learn how to maximize the power of the search interface.

- The scope of the searchable collection is visibly identified and clearly described on the search interface page so that users know which area of the site they are searching.

- The search results page is clearly organized and information is thoroughly presented so that users can easily make selection decisions and not have to sort through redundant, vague, and incomplete result links.

- Each page is clearly labeled with a header, date, and source so that users have landmarks and a sense of where they are.

- Menu options are limited to five to seven choices unless they are grouped as a chunk of information so that users can absorb information.

- Links are underlined in blue for consistency, and a phrase instead of a word is underlined so that users can recognize links and have more information on which to base a linking decision.

- Links have meaningful and obvious labels; abstraction is avoided so that users do not have to second-guess each link's meaning.

- Alternative methods of navigation exist, including navigational bars at the bottom and top of the page, so that users have increased control over interaction with the interface at all times.

- Consistency exists throughout, especially in layout, icons, terminology, and placement of options and color, so that users can apply what they have learned from page to page.

- Graphics are kept at a minimum and appear only when they add valuable meaning to the content on the screen.

- Animation is used very sparingly, if at all, so that users' distraction levels are decreased and they can concentrate on information retrieval tasks.

- Downloading time for graphics is minimized by showing thumbnails that have an option for enlargement.

- "Alt text" tags give users the option to avoid images altogether but still know their meaning.

- Pages are laid out so that white space and barriers (e.g., horizontal lines) are at a minimum so that the content is easily scanned by users.

- Web writing is concise and objective, instead of promotional, so that users can process content quickly.

- Pages with text do not exceed two to three full screens so that users can scan the content quickly.

- Users receive feedback about image size, loading time, and processing time so they know whether the system is working.

- Users have the option to contact the Webmaster with a "mail to" function and can expect a timely response.

Table 5.8 *The Pick of the Lot: Recommended Readings and Web Sites*

- Janet Cottrell and Michael B. Eisenberg, "Web Design for Information Problem-Solving: Maximizing Value for Users." *Computers in Libraries*, vol. 17, no. 5, May 1997, pp. 52–7.

- Kate Ehrlich. "So You Wanna Design for the Web?" *interactions*, (ACM journal), March 1996, pp. 19–23.

- Patrick J. Lynch and Sarah Horton. "Designing Reference Sites for the Web." *Yale C/AIM WWW Style Guide*, 1997, http://www.info.med.yale.edu/caim/manual/contents.html. Also look for a soon-to-be-published book by Lynch and Horton—a resource with great promise: *Web Style Guide*, New Haven, Conn.: Yale University Press, 1999.

- Louis Rosenfield and Peter Morville, *Information Architecture for the World Wide Web*, Sebastopol, Calif.: O'Reilly, 1998.

- Jared M. Spool, Tara Scanlon, Will Schroeder, Carolyn Snyder, and Terri DeAngelo, *Web Usability: A Designer's Guide*, User Interface Engineering, Andover, Mass., 1997.

- Eric Bergman and Earl Johnson, "Towards Accessible Human-Computer Interaction," in Jakob Nielsen, ed., *Advances in Human Computer Interaction*, Norwood, N.J.: Ablex Publishing, vol. 5, 1995. Also available on Sun's Technology and Research site at: http://www.sun.com/tech/access/updt.HCI.advance.html.

- Sheryl Burgstahler, Dan Comden, and Beth Fraser, "Universal Access: Designing and Evaluating Web Sites for Accessibility," *CHOICE*, vol. 34, Supplement 1997, pp. 19–22.

- Eric Christierson and Donna Pontau, "Universal Design for Library Web Pages: Providing Access for Users with Disabilities," San Jose State University Faculty Diversity Grant Project Report, 1998. (For more information about the school's center, see http://www.drc.sjsu.edu.)

- Courtney Deines-Jones, "EASI Access to Library Technology," *Library Hi Tech News*, June 1997, pp. 18–31.

- Trace Research and Development Center. University of Wisconsin at Madison, http://www.trace.wisc.edu.

- Web Accessibility Initiative (WAI) at http://www.w3.org/WAI/.

INSIDE . . .

An Interview with Lou Rosenfeld About Web Design for Information Retrieval

Lou Rosenfeld is co-author with Peter Morville of Information Architecture for the World Wide Web *(1998); a columnist for* Web Review *magazine; and president of Argus Associates, (http://www.argus-inc.com) an information architecture and Web development firm with clients that include Borders Books and Music, AT&T, and Chrysler Corporation.*

People regularly complain about trying to find information on the Web. What is at the root of most of these problems?

Information retrieval is difficult in any medium. If you look at some of the studies evaluating information retrieval performance in traditional information systems, you'll find that information retrieval works really poorly, in general, in those situations. And I'm talking about fairly homogenous collections of content with a handful of formats and a specific set of queries within a specific domain and dealing with specific audiences. But when you take the Web, which is highly heterogeneous, in all senses of the word—from types of content to types of users to the domain covered to how people are going to use this information—you end up with this horrible apples and oranges problem, where information retrieval is going to perform much worse than anything in a traditional environment. Here's the basic rule: Information retrieval works better the more you can narrow the focus, the more you can separate the apples from the oranges. The only way the Web will perform well is if developers actively try to re-partition content, types of uses, and types of users in new ways.

What are terrible Web sites to someone like you?

Terrible sites for me are self-centered sites. The intent of these sites may be to serve users but, in practicality, the truth is that it is self-aggrandizement or self-exploration. I mean in terms of "I'm going to put a counter on my page! Look everyone, I can put a counter on my page and it works!" This adds absolutely no value for the user or the owner of the site. This used to bother me more. But in a broader context, I've come to realize that it's just a way for people to learn how to use a new medium. But serious businesses doing things like that, really trashing their own images and not serving their prospective client—I just don't understand it. It reveals a total lack of understanding of this medium. I'm turned off by it because it is not user-centric.

Then, more seriously, are the sites that are fairly well developed but then again squeeze everyone into the same hole—square pegs, round pegs— all fitting into the same hole. There is no understanding that their users are not all alike. Even if they have the same types of users coming to their site, depending on the users' information needs, the users may need to find and use information very differently from time to time. It frustrates me when companies in the information business offer only one interface for all users to use.

Your company has worked on Web sites for some big clients. As a developer, do you assume certain things about how potential users might look for information on the Web?

I'm extremely uncomfortable making assumptions about users, but there is a practicality to it. Often clients say, "Yeah, yeah, user testing . . . but we need to get a site up now!" It's hard to make a case for testing. But we have still taken an approach for interviewing people that are at least in touch with their organization's users. We try to learn a little bit about users and their differing information needs. We then try to present differing means for finding information in the site.

We tell clients that most sites don't even address 50 percent of their users' information needs. We are going to represent 80 percent of what we think will be possible information needs. If we went with 100 percent, it would be impossible, we would get pages that were cluttered and overwhelming and then the site wouldn't work for anyone. To accomplish our goal, we work in methods of searching, variants on searching, different means of browsing that range from browsing by topic or by audience or by tasks, table of contents versus indices. There's a wide palette of ways that we can support users' efforts to find information. Hopefully, we have staying power with the client and then we can, over time, figure out which ones are actually working for users.

What exactly do you mean by information architecture, the topic of your latest book about the Web?

Information architecture is about Web sites and other information systems and supporting information retrieval. This is done by having certain foundations for organizing information—how you label it, what you call it, how you might have ways for information to be navigated, and how it might be searched. Information architecture goes beyond navigation, but a huge issue is information searching through retrieval. Also, there are broader issues about designing systems so that they map to the mental models of users. In other words, when someone comes to a Web site, they need good information architecture so that they can understand what that information is about, who it is for, and what it is supposed to do for them. So before they plunge into trying to navigate or search, they need to have a bigger-picture idea about what this thing is and why it is there for them to use.

Which sites do a good job at supporting information retrieval tasks?

Northern Light comes to mind. They do simple things like grouping results. It may not be what I want all of the time, but it is helpful. HotBot is good, too, because it is clear what you are searching. Dividing up the realm of content into specific search zones—Usenets versus the Web versus this versus that—is an important and basic principle that we are seeing more and more of now. But I don't like the complexity of their advanced interface. Along with their simplified interface, it feels like you either get nothing or you get everything imaginable. I'd like to see more of a gradual continuum. The search interfaces also vary from other ones I've used; the consistency with other kinds out there would make them easier to use. Not that interfaces should be the same for every site, but, when possible, make things work and behave more consistently, as long as it doesn't compromise the functionality.

Endnotes

1. Roger Fidler, *Mediamorphosis*, Thousand Oaks, Calif.: Pine Forge Press, 1997, pp. 101–5.
2. J. Pitkow and C. Kehoe, *GVU's 4th World-Wide Web User Survey*, Georgia Institute of Technology. Available http://www.cc.gatech.edu/gvu/user_surveys/survey-10-1995/. 19 Feb. 1999.

3. Ben Shneiderman, "Is the Web Really Different from Everything Else?" *CHI 98: Human Factors in Computing Systems*, New York: Association for Computing Machinery, CHI 98 Summary, ACM Conference Proceedings, p. 92.

4. Jared M. Spool, Tara Scanlon, Will Schroeder, Carolyn Snyder, and Terri DeAngelo, *Web Usability: A Designer's Guide*, Andover, Mass.: User Interface Engineering, 1997, p. 12.

5. "Usability Testing of World Wide Web Sites," *SIGCHI WWW SIA: CHI 97*, ACM Conference, notes from the session are posted on the Web. Available http://www.acm.org/sigchi/web/chi97testing/ricknote.htm. 19 Feb. 1999.

6. J. Pitkow and C. Kehoe, *GVU's 6th World-Wide Web User Survey*, Georgia Institute of Technology. Available http://www.cc.gatech.edu/gvu/user_surveys/survey-10-1996/. 19 Feb. 1999.

7. Conversation with Albert Sears while he was employed as a news researcher at *The Santa Rosa Press Democrat* Newspaper in 1995.

8. Laurie Kanter and Stephanie Rosenbaum, "Usability Studies of WWW Sites: Heuristic Evaluation vs. Laboratory Testing," *SIGDOC 97*, Snowbird, Utah, New York: Association for Computing Machinery, ACM Conference Proceedings, 1997.

9. Jared Sandberg, "Dull-Data Sites Become Shining Stars of the Web," *Wall Street Journal* article as it appeared in *The Santa Rosa Press Democrat*, July 26, 1998, p. E1.

10. Jakob Nielsen, "User Interface Design for the WWW," *CHI 97 Proceedings*. Available http://www.acm.org/sigchi/chi97/proceedings/tutorial/jn.htm. 19 Feb. 1999.

11. Linda Tauscher and Saul Greenberg, "Revisitation Patterns in World Wide Web Navigation," *CHI 97 Proceedings*, ACM Conference Proceedings, 1997, p. 399.

12. Spool, op. cit., p. 87.

13. Spool, op. cit., p. 11.

14. Patrick J. Lynch and Sarah Horton, "Designing Reference Sites for the Web," *Yale C/AIM WWW Style Guide*. Available http://www.info.med.yale.edu/caim/manual/contents.html. 19 Feb. 1999.

15. Spool, op. cit., p. 18.

16. Ibid.

17. Spool, op. cit., p. 28.

18. Spool, op. cit., pp. 47–56.

19. Spool, op. cit., pp. 51–5.

20. David Rothenberg, "How the Web Destroys the Quality of Students' Research Papers," *Chronicle of Higher Education*, August 15, 1997, p. A44.

21. Louis Rosenfeld and Peter Morville, *Information Architecture for the World Wide Web*, Sebastopol, Calif.: O'Reilly, 1998, pp. 101–3.

22. Spool, op. cit., p. 14.

23. Spool, op. cit., pp. 14-7.

24. Amy Kanerva, Kevin Keeker, Kirsten Risden, Eric Schuh, and Mary Czerwinski, "Web Usability Research at Microsoft Corporation," in Chris Forsythe, Eric Grose, and Julie Ratner, eds., *Human Factors and Web Development*, Mahwah, N.J.: Lawrence Erlbaum Publishers, 1998, p. 193.

25. Jared Spool, "Surprises on the Web," *User Interface Engineering Newsletter*, Oct. 1996. Available http://world.std.com/~uieweb/surprise.htm. 19 Feb. 1999.

26. Ibid.

27. Hal Shubin and Ron Perkins, "Web Navigation: Resolving Conflicts Between the Desktop and the Web," *CHI 98 Summary*, New York: Association for Computing Machinery, ACM Conference Proceedings, 1998, p. 209.

28. Eric Grose, Chris Forsythe, and Julie Ratner, "Using Interfaces and Traditional Style Guides to Design Interfaces," in *Human Factors and Web Development*, Chris Forsythe, Eric Grose, and Julie Ratner, eds., Mahwah, N.J.: Lawrence Erlbaum Publishers, 1998, p. 123.

29. Jose A. Borges, Israel Morales, and Nestor J. Rodriguez, "Guidelines for Designing Usable World Wide Web Pages," *CHI 96 Companion*, New York: Association for Computing Machinery, ACM Conference Proceedings, 1996, p. 277.

30. Spool, op. cit., *Web Usability*, p. 42.

31. Nielsen, op. cit., "User Interface Design for the WWW."

32. Jakob Nielsen, "Is the Web Really Different from Everything Else?" *CHI 98: Human Factors in Computing Systems, CHI 98 Summary*, New York: Association for Computing Machinery, ACM Conference Proceedings, 1998, p. 93.

33. David Siegel, *Secrets of Successful Web Sites: Project Management on the World Wide Web*, Indianapolis: Hayden Books, 1997.

34. Patrick Lynch and Sarah Horton, "Design Standards," *Yale C/AIM Web Style Guide*. Available http://www.info.med.yale.edu/caim/manual/sites/intranet_design.html. 19 Feb. 1999.

35. The Sun story as cited in Patrick Lynch and Sarah Horton, "Navigation: Time Is Money," op. cit., Yale *C/AIM Web Style Guide*.

36. Ibid.

37. "Usability Testing of World Wide Web Sites," op. cit.

38. Eric N. Weibe and Julie E. Howe, "Graphics Design on the Web," in Chris Forsythe, Eric Grose, and Julie Ratner, eds., *Human Factors and Web Development*, Mahwah, N.J.: Lawrence Erlbaum Publishers, 1998, p. 235.

39. Pitkow and Kehoe, op. cit., *GVU's 6th Survey*

40. Rothenberg, op. cit.

41. Spool, op. cit., *Web Usability*, p. 18.

42. Kanerva et al., op. cit., p. 193.

43. Ibid.

44. Ibid.

45. *Sun's Guide to Web Style.* Available http://www.sun.com/styleguide/tables/ Navigation.html. 19 Feb. 1999.
46. Spool, op. cit., *Web Usability*, pp. 20–7.
47. M. E. Morris and R. J. Hinrichs, *Web Page Design: A Different Multimedia*, Upper Saddle, N.J.: Prentice-Hall, 1996.
48. Lynch and Horton, op. cit., "Design Standards."
49. Thomas Weber, "E-Mail Queries Confound Companies," *The Wall Street Journal* article as it appeared in *The Santa Rosa Press Democrat*, October 28, 1996, p. E1.
50. Pamela Licalzi O'Connell, "Black Hole of E-Mail: Web Messages Like 2nd-Class Communication," *New York Times* article as it appeared in *The Santa Rosa Press Democrat*, July 10, 1998, p. E1.
51. Jennifer Fleming, "In Defense of Web Graphics: Graphic Designers Offer More Than Just Flashy Graphics," *Web Review*, July 25, 1997. Also available http:// webreview.com/wr/pub/97/07/25/feature/index4.html. 19 Feb. 1999.
52. Lynch and Horton, "Build Clear Navigation Aids." *Yale C/AIM WWW Style Guide.* Available http://www.info.med.yale.edu/caim/manual/contents.html. 19 Feb. 1999.
53. *Sun's Guide to Web Style*, op. cit., "Purposes."
54. Spool, op. cit., *Web Usability*, p. 7.
55. Ibid.
56. Lynch and Horton, op. cit., "Build Clear Navigation Aids."
57. Spool, op. cit., *Web Usability*, p. 88.
58. Chris Johnson, "The Ten Golden Rules for Providing Video over the Web or 0% of 2.4M (at 270k/sec, 340 sec Remaining)," in Chris Forsythe, Eric Grose, and Julie Ratner, eds., *Human Factors and Web Development*, Mahwah, N.J.: Lawrence Erlbaum Publishers, 1998, p. 208.
59. *Sun's Guide to Web Style*, op. cit., "Graphics." (Slightly modified, as it appears here, for clarity).
60. Richard C. Omanson, Gavin S. Lew, and Robert M. Schumacher, "Creating Content for Both Paper and the Web," (Readability studies cited: Gould and Grischkowsky, 1984; Muter, Latremouille, Treurniet, and Beam, 1982; and Wright and Likorish, 1983), in Chris Forsythe, Eric Grose, and Julie Ratner, eds., *Human Factors and Web Development*, Mahwah, N.J.: Lawrence Erlbaum Publishers, 1998, p. 201.
61. Spool, op. cit., *Web Usability*, p. 68.
62. John Morkes and Jakob Nielsen, "Applying Writing Guidelines to Web Pages," *CHI 98 Summary*, New York: Association for Computing Machinery, ACM Press, 1998, p. 321.
63. Kanerva et al., op. cit., p. 194.
64. Ibid.
65. Spool, op. cit., *Web Usability*, p. 74.
66. Beverly B. Zimmerman, "Applying Tufte's Principles of Information Design to Creating Effective Web Pages," *SIGDOC 97*, ACM Conference Proceedings, Snowbird, Utah, New York: Association for Computing Machinery, 1997.

67. Morkes and Nielsen, op. cit., p. 321.

68. Morkes and Nielsen, op. cit., p. 322.

69. Eric Bergman and Earl Johnson, "Towards Accessible Human-Computer Interaction," in Jakob Nielsen, ed., *Advances in Human Computer Interaction*, Norwood, N.J.: Ablex Publishing, vol. 5, 1995. Also available on Sun's Technology and Research Web site: http://www.sun.com/tech/access/updt.HCI.advance.html. 21 Feb. 1999. (Bergman and Johnson cite H. H. Perritt's *The Americans with Disabilities Act Handbook*, 2nd ed., New York: John Wiley and Sons, 1991.)

70. Bergman and Johnson, op. cit. The authors cite J. Elkind, "The Incidence of Disabilities in the United States," *Human Factors*, vol. 32, no. 4, 1990, pp. 397–405.

71. Bergman and Johnson, op. cit. The authors cite G. C. Vanderheiden, "Thirty-Something Million: Should They be Exceptions?" *Human Factors*, vol. 32, no. 4, 1990, pp. 383–96.

72. Bergman and Johnson, op. cit.

73. Bergman and Johnson, op. cit. The authors cite W. W. McMillan, "Computing for Users with Special Needs and Models of Computer-Human Interaction." *CHI '92 Proceedings*, 1992, pp. 143–8.

74. McMillan, op. cit., pp. 143–8.

75. Bergman and Johnson, op. cit.

76. *Sun Microsystem's Enabling Technologies Web Page*, http://www.sun.com/tech/access/access.quick.ref.html.

77. Bergman and Johnson, op. cit.

78. For a full account of disabilities that affect computer users and design solutions for accessibility, see Eric Bergman and Earl Johnson, "Designing for Accessibility," Sun Microsystems' Technology and Research Page. Available http://www.sun.com/tech/access/. 21 Feb. 1999

79. For more information on how computer systems and assistive technologies can help people with different disabilities, see The Alliance for Technology Access's *Computer Resources for People with Disabilities*, Alameda, Calif.: Hunter House, 1996.

80. Eric Christierson and Donna Pontau, "Universal Design for Library Web Pages: Providing Access for Users with Disabilities," San Jose State University Faculty Diversity Grant Project, 1998.

81. Ibid.

82. Bergman and Johnson, op. cit.

83. Joseph Lazzaro, "Designing for a Wider Universe," *Web Review*, Sept. 4, 1998. Also available http://webreview.com/wr/pub/98/09/04/feature/index2.html. 21 Feb. 1999.

84. Comment relayed during the field testing of cnn.com with Eric Christierson on Sept. 8, 1998.

85. For more information, refer to the ADA home page. Available http://www.usdoj.gov/crt/ada/. 21 Feb. 1999.

86. Lazzaro, op. cit.

87. This checklist is a compilation, which was drawn from my own research and thoughts about Web design for users with special needs and from the evaluation of checklists developed in Burgstahler, Sheryl, Dan Comden, and Beth Fraser, "Universal Access: Designing and Evaluating Web Sites for Accessibility," *CHOICE*, vol. 34, supplement, 1997, pp. 19–22; Deines-Jones, Courtney, "EASI Access to Library Technology," *Library Hi Tech News*, June 1997, pp. 18–31; Paciello, Mike, and Yuri Rubinsky, "Making the Web Accessible for the Deaf, Hearing and Mobility Impaired," 1996. Available http://www.samizdat.com/pac2.html. 21 Feb. 1999; Kautzman, Amy, "Virtuous, Virtual Access: Making Web Pages Accessible to People with Disabilities," *Searcher*, June 1998, pp. 42–7.

88. The Bobby site and testing program [online]. Available http://www.cast.org/bobby. 21 Feb. 1999.

89. Lynch and Horton, "Web Pages Versus Conventional Document Design." Available http://www.info.med.yale.edu/caim/manual/interface/interface.html. 21 Feb. 1999.

90. This checklist is a compilation, which was drawn from my own research and thoughts about Web design for information retrieval and from the evaluation of checklists developed in Spool, *Web Usability*, op. cit.; Lynch and Horton, *Yale C/AIM WWW Style Guide*. Available http://www.info.med.yale.edu/caim/manual/contents. html. 19 Feb. 1999; *Sun's Guide to Web Style*, op. cit.; Janet Cottrell and Michael B. Eisenberg, "Web Design for Information Problem-Solving: Maximizing Value for Users," *Computers in Libraries*, vol. 17, no. 5, May 1997, pp. 52–7; and Morkes and Nielsen, op. cit., pp. 321–22.

91. Edward Tufte, *Envisioning Information*, Cheshire, Conn.: Graphics Press, 1990, p. 9.

Note: Date following Web citations indicates date of access.

6
Online Commercial Databases: Power Tools Unplugged?

The names Dialog, Nexis, and Dow Jones are legendary in information professional circles. These are just three of the powerful online services that are fee-based, precision research tools used for accessing an abundance of continually expanding full-text sources, which range from Appellate Court decisions and 10K financial statements to newspaper and scholarly journal articles. Due to their uniformly *user-unfriendly* command line interface designs, though, access to the systems has long been kept under lock and password in most libraries' back offices. When it came to inputting esoteric commands, power searchers needed to possess the exacting composure of a carnival knife thrower.

But in the mid-1990s, everything began to change. A majority of the online services demystified their interface design, reworking arcane command systems into friendlier GUIs that provided a range of services that were soon ported to the Web. Promoting intuitive Web graphical interfaces, the online service providers counted on luring a greater percentage of end users who were not professional researchers but still had a need for highly valued information they could quickly and easily locate. All at once, online

Design in a Nutshell

For years, online commercial services were the ultimate power tool. These highly specialized research systems attracted a small band of professional searchers, mostly librarians, who diligently learned the esoteric commands of each command line system in order to carry out their tasks—mining and manipulating the full-text content of megadatabases. What has always mattered to power searchers is whether the underlying structure of databases is integrally tied to the system's search capabilities. Power searchers often evaluate a system's effectiveness by examining its capacity for precision searching.

But in the 1990s, the majority of the command systems morphed. First, the old command style interfaces were reworked into graphical interface remakes. Shortly thereafter, many of the newly fabricated GUIs migrated to the Web where they became known as *Web databases*. The Web interface held the promises for power searchers of multimedia capabilities, increased accessibility, and a more intuitive design. For the providers, Web databases meant a more reliable operating platform than their previous anachronistic mainframe systems and a shot at tapping a growing end-user business market.

The GUI remakes have delivered an interface that is more focused on supporting *usability* than on delivering *task support*. In product reviews of Web databases, expert searchers consistently lament the loss of processing speed and search capabilities. End users seek other features from Web databases: They want more intelligence built into the systems so they are not overloaded with data and quick answers to their research questions. Whether Web databases can keep both user bases happy—even with separate Web products—remains to be seen. Part of the providers' success depends on how well their GUI designs communicate to their user base. So far, the aesthetics of Web databases are bound by the constraints of Web design: Information retrieval consists of form-filling, which works for known-item searching but suffers at helping users develop strategies for more abstract information gathering. Web databases are susceptible to clutter; each screen typically supports a browser's navigational buttons, the search interface's navigational bar, and the page's content. Not surprisingly, Web databases that succeed with users have a simplified design that is primarily focused on supporting information retrieval tasks.

services began to move out of the shadows of reference libraries and into the hands of end users.

Design Analysis
Task Support: Caught Between Two Masters

There is little doubt that online commercial databases were originally developed as an information retrieval tool for experts. In 1964, one of the first online systems was in development at Lockheed Missiles and Space Company for use as an internal research resource.[1] Several years later, Lockheed launched a commercial version of the modified system, which they called Dialog, and it quickly became an information industry standard. Dialog and a handful of other online service competitors that soon followed supported highly focused research tasks by providing users with capabilities for quickly cutting through vast amounts of data.

The providers, however, faced difficulties with converting proprietary systems into commercial ventures. Their complicated pricing models showed it.[2] Users were separately charged for their searching, downloading, and telecommunications costs. Under these conditions, expenditures could quickly mount, especially when the systems were used by beginners or casual users that were unfamiliar with the commands for each system.[3] Not surprisingly, commercial online databases soon ended up in the toolbox of trained and qualified searchers, mostly librarians, partly out of need but also because of the potentially high costs associated with their operation.

When it comes to task support and the effectiveness of the databases' command line searching interfaces, little has been written. Most of the literature consists of product reviews that focus on how readily power searchers can manipulate competing systems to quickly and inexpensively complete research tasks.[4] *Power searching*, in the professional researcher's vernacular, means the process of partitioning and honing voluminous content. A power searcher's typical strategy is to cast a large net, a megafile search, and then to use his or her mastery with powerful commands to refine results through iterative searching. Unique commands, like proximity operators (a device for ferreting out multiple occurrences of keywords that appear near one another), are the essential tools of power searchers.[5] Beyond a searcher's skills, at the heart of every well-designed system is *data integration*:

> The primary question about all proprietary search software remains whether it's just a "front end," a pretty face that sits on top of the data and re-expresses some of the underlying command language and syntax in menu or other allegedly easy-to-use forms, or whether the software—and the search capabilities and options it embodies—are intimately integrated with the underlying data. Designing software of the latter type usually involves some redesigning of the data structures, and sometimes even of the hardware platform itself.[6]

In short, expert level task support hinges on three interface components: (1) the availability, consistency, and flexibility of precision commands that enable a database's content to be manipulated; (2) content that is logically organized into relevant subfiles that are likely to be accessed; and (3) processing speed.

For years, command online services played to a small cadre of expert searchers willing to learn the powerful commands and to remember under which circumstances they were best applied. But then in the mid-1990s, a majority of commercial online providers did an about-face. Command systems were all but replaced by GUIs. Soon thereafter, many of these GUI systems were ported to the Web, delivering GUI/command hybrid interfaces that became known as *Web databases.*[7] Part of the transformation was hastened by market pressure from online expert searchers. One professional searcher writing about online services and the Web wrote as late as 1996:

> The traditional database industry is still not with the program. The Internet is going to hit it like a freight train. You have all the data, all the content, and you come late to the party.[8]

Much of the impetus for developing Web databases was grounded in entrepreneurial opportunities. A Web platform proved to be fortuitous for online services. The platform presented a multimedia environment that goes well beyond full text and introduces a flexible infrastructure that can be upgraded far more easily than previously existing proprietary systems.[9] The Web also has huge revenue-making potential. Online services can now go after a vast end-user market that, until the Web, has remained largely untapped. One online service industry veteran estimated as long ago as 1995 that there are 16 million PCs with modems in business settings, representing a market to online services that is potentially worth $2 billion in the U.S. and $5 to $6 billion worldwide.[10] These amounts have only increased.

Despite the marketing allure, converting a command system into a GUI is no easy design feat. Some services have made the jump effortlessly, while others have failed miserably, making the design evaluation process complex and uneven. At the core of the conversion process is task support. How can the GUI hybrids support the information retrieval tasks of both sets of users, experts and end users? Without a doubt, there are particular problems associated with designing an interface for a broad and amorphous end-user base and its constituents' diverse information-seeking needs. One information industry analyst writes that part of the problem is:

> There is no set of "generic" needs or capabilities shared by all business information users. In addition to specific industry or job function needs, end users vary in their awareness, motivation, and capability when it comes to online (and offline) business information.[11]

Evaluators should be weary of a system that tries to meet the task support needs of a new population of end users. For the most part, a system that only accommodates novices first and foremost is shortsighted. Beginners are likely to become intermediate and even expert users over time, who have different expectations from a system. Building flexibility into interfaces, especially shortcuts, allows for users to grow in proficiency with a given system. Ultimately, all users want the same basic capability from fee-based Web databases: processing speed. Beyond that, though, there is great divergence about what end users expect from systems and what experts want. End users, who are often also casual users, tend to want features that include:

- Integrated plug-and-play installation

- Context-sensitive, online help (not manuals)

- Navigational devices that work harder at giving users answers instead of merely data

• Straightforward menus instead of commands

• Built-in intelligence for processing requests

• Full text, graphics, and tables

• No penalties for their inexperience[12]

As the listing implies, catering to the information retrieval tasks of end users means creating more invisibility in interfaces. Some critics argue that the only way that Web databases will survive in the end-user market is by becoming *decision bases*. Decision bases deliver value-added content to users and solve information problems by reducing the need for users to hedge their information-seeking strategies.[13] This calls for a system that is, in particular, supported by extensive and consistent indexing. Extensive thesauri are a necessary component, linking data behind the scenes and making systems more intelligent. Unfortunately, this level of translation is something few systems already have programmed into place. In fact, most online commercial providers have long acted as middlemen, selling content that is indexed by the source that provides the data to them. This practice does little for creating overall consistency in indexing. Design problems and issues are compounded by the other large segment of potential users, experts, who have an entirely different set of expectations when it comes to task support and Web databases. At first glance, Web databases give veteran searchers what they have long craved:

• Increases in accessibility

• Freedom from dedicated equipment

• Lower telecommunications connect-rates

• Graphical capabilities

• Online documentation

• Hypertext linking in otherwise closed, proprietary systems[14]

Table 6.1 Favorable Features: Web Databases and Traditional Online Services

Web Database Services	Traditional Online Systems
• User-friendly interfaces	• Greater reliability of the system
• Value-added features, including graphical capabilities	• More potential for manipulating data
• Linking to other sites and analytical reviews	• Immediate access to a supermarket of databases without trying to locate speciality database sources
• Some free features (e.g., documentation, browsing)	• Greater precision in searching
• More affordable rates	• Greater productivity when quick access to large amounts is required seven days a week
• Decision bases	• Option to use a Web-based version of the system

Source: Amelia Kassel, "Here They Come!: Database Producers on the Web," *Searcher*, vol. 5, no. 7, June 1997, p. 35.

Table 6.1 provides a product review recap of the more favorable features offered in both Web databases and traditional online systems.[15]

Do not be mistaken, though, there are disadvantages for power searchers using Web databases, too. At the heart of the design matter is user interaction. One professional researcher describes the differences between using a version of the provider's command interface versus a GUI version of the same basic system:

There are times when a good searcher really gets "in the zone" when doing a search—you try an idea, you see how it plays, you tweak it a bit or try a slightly different riff and see what comes out—it's like good improvisational jazz or the Grateful Dead on a good night. This kind of almost seamless interaction between the searcher and the data is easy to slip into with command-line searching. It's almost impossible on the Web—instead of feeling like I'm playing an instrument, I feel like I'm lugging a weight around. Push. Yank. Wait. Scroll down to see where I am. Wait. It works, but music it's not.[16]

Even though a majority of Web databases have aptly offered two levels of search interfaces in one system (command/advanced and guided/simple) or at least two separate products for each user base, there is little question that task support for power users has fundamentally changed on the Web. As Anne Mintz (who is interviewed at the end of this chapter) points out, the repertoire of specialized commands for manipulating data, which gave power searchers a lot of their juice, has not been fully carried forward into many of the Web database remakes. An oft-cited example comes from Dialog Web, which did not initially include the ability to stack commands in their Web database remake.[17]

Another important evaluation issue is that productivity has decreased with the comparative slowness of Web databases. One of the earlier versions of Dialog Web makes users wait until one set is completely processed before another command will be accepted. This outcome did not occur with their command predecessor. Overall, a handful of information industry product reviews found fault with a majority of initial Web databases releases for these reasons:

- Taking too long to search

- Prohibiting multiple databases searching

- Offering reduced search and field options

- Providing limited range of output choices[18,19]

According to one expert, using the Web version of Dialog actually slows her analytical abilities—how she thinks online—as a searcher.[20] Users' processing pace is too quick for the Web databases, which is a problem that came up in the following field test of Dialog Web.

Field Test: Dialog Web

(http://www.dialogweb.com)

I admit I am an old-time power searcher. I think in Boolean terms, treasuring the rhythms and interplay of logic, set manipulation, and intuition that is part of classic command-line searching. But, as an academic librarian, I also work in an environment where end-user searching is a goal, and I spend considerable time helping novices navigate online systems. Right up front, Dialog Web announces itself as a product that presumes knowledge of Dialog command language, but I need to investigate further as to whether there is enough flexibility for the Web database to support the tasks of a mixed user base of experts and novices.

First, how does Dialog Web look to users when they initially log-on? The layout is clean and clear, and the functions that users of all levels need most (especially links to searching) are front and center. The colors, graphics, and organization of the pages help focus attention on the business at hand. Every page has access to cost, help, and the all-important exit from the system, which users of all levels appreciate in a design. Another plus is that power users can head to Dialog Web's command mode and be on familiar ground. The visuals of the Web interface do not get in the way. The page fits on my small monitor, and, even if I minimize the size of the browser, I can still see the essentials. The trade-off is that the command input box for search terms is small. If I type in a long search, the beginning of my search terms scroll off to the left of the screen, making it difficult to look for "typos." So far, the layout visually conveys that I can do most, if not all, of what I used to be able to do in the command version of Dialog without wrapping myself around a hypertext axle of user-friendly embellishments.

But when it comes to *actually using* Dialog Web, it is *sooo* slow. I find myself counting under my breath, urging the system on as my requests are processed. In the interim, at least I can see that something is happening; the center of the screen clears and a message appears, telling me that the system is working. When you use the Web, you deal with the Web's response time, but it's hard to keep a feeling of being engaged in the search process during those long absences. As a searcher familiar with the classic Dialog, I noticeably miss the pace and the rhythms of the old interface style. The question remains: Why bother using Dialog Web if I search it just like the classic command line version of Dialog at a faster rate?

With Dialog Web, there are enhanced features; some nice online assistance is built into the system that is useful for beginning or intermediate searchers, or experts who are new to a particular set of databases. If online help is needed, it is available at no cost. The overall pricing structure is different, too; there are no connect charges while you are linked to help screens. There are links to tutorials, search and printing helps, and database information. (I like the use of the blue background on the database information sheets; it mimics the "blue sheet" of the paper descriptions, and gives a nice sense of familiarity in the Web environment.) Plus, the Web database interface is flexible; I can get help to discover what to do next, but am left free to use commands.

How might a novice searcher approach this system? Let's say I am new to online searching and need to find information on a fairly specific topic.

There are three search options with Dialog Web: a Guided Search; an Expert Search; and the tempting Databases option, which promises free searching to sort out which databases are available. As a novice, if I choose Databases, I would be in for a surprise. I have to use Dialog commands to search. If I do not comply, then there's a polite message that I have neglected to enter a Dialog command, but at least there is a link to a help screen that explains the search syntax I need to use. I can persist and continue making my way through the Database guide with the assistance of the help screens, or I might choose to go directly to the Guided Search in hopes of avoiding command language.

The first screen in Guided Search is a list of categories of databases—News & Media, Reference, etc. My question, "How do I know which to use?" is anticipated by the design. There's an Expand Categories option centered just below the list. The system continues to lead me through a series of choices to select my databases. I enter my search (there's help on the same page that describes the various choices) and await the results. Reviewing my search results gets me deeper into unknown territory. (What's this "sort s 1/all/pd, d" stuff mean? What are these buttons for "tags," "bluesheets," and "fields"?) I make a long detour to the help screens. Later, I display two items from my retrieval in full-text format. Then, I wait. And I wait some more. I wander away from the computer and into the kitchen and pour myself some coffee. (There is a lesson here. This is not a productive system if you have a slow Internet connection.)

Shortly after my return, I get my full-text displays. The articles are okay, but I want to revise my search a bit. Surprise. There is nowhere that says "new search" or "modify search." I have to either enter a Dialog command or go back to the beginning and work my way through all the database choice screens. There is a work-around to avoid this shortcoming of the design. I can use the back button on my browser to get back to my search screen, but I am going to have to figure that one out on my own. Revising my search and trying again, I find a number of interesting articles; work my way through the print/save options (easy enough, but this requires that I am familiar with the browser's print and save functions); come away from the search with some success; and, probably, I am not too frustrated with the process.

Testing from both an expert and novice perspective shows that Dialog Web is an interface that is still being developed and, at best, is a compromise. Unfortunately, Dialog Web will not make the die-hard power searcher happy (especially with the system's slow response time and tried-and-true precision commands). Dialog Web is not for the absolute novice, either (there's an assumption of familiarity with basic terms). So far, its major plus is the flexibility of the system. You can get away with using the design with a minimum of knowledge, and as you learn the system, it allows you more and more freedom.

Field testing of Dialog Web, Version 1.2.1 was performed on September 15, 1998, by Elisabeth Green, San Jose State University Graduate School of Library and Information Science and Stanford University Libraries.

Usability: Trade-Offs and Priorities

For almost 20 years, command style interfaces won the devotion of expert searchers but, at the same time, created little confidence among novices. Ambiguous commands, poor error-handling abilities, slowness of mainframe systems, and a design that offered little forgiveness or feedback helped to foster great resistance among users who were trying to learn the systems. Novices tended to be infrequent users who were easily stymied over choosing which database to search—long before searching for content began.[21] Command systems were exclusively expert tools; delivering usability to novices was the farthest thing from system developers' minds.

Not surprisingly, much of the success experts experienced with online services was derived from their familiarity with a system, rather than from the interface design itself.[22] If users had the tenacity to master the basics—the esoteric command language and the necessary strategies for information retrieval—the floodgates opened up wide. Multiple databases from the same provider could be stacked and searched in one fell swoop; output could be ranked and customized with a single command. Other features included an online thesaurus, truncation, natural language, and free text searching.[23] But usability turned on a number of factors besides the obstacles associated with learning a command language.[24] A usable system for power searchers is a patchwork of perceptions, derived from which system was learned first, which one is used with ongoing frequency, and how much knowledge users have about the searching domain.[25] In other words, experts have long considered individual systems that they frequently use and that they have mastered to be *usable*.

Still, the lack of consistent commands across systems—from Dialog to Nexis to Dow Jones—was a usability sticking point for years among many information professionals before the GUI remakes. Some searchers argued for consistent commands, which would make switching between systems easier and also reduce their own need for memorization. But the plea was mostly ignored by the providers. And it may have been a blessing. From a design point of view, consistency across systems would have been a mistake. Consistency may support learning and lessen the need for memorization, but, at the same time, consistency across systems could have impeded the precision of the tools upon which experts so heavily relied. If the online services had attempted to deliver standardization, systems would have had to be reconfigured based on their similarities. The lowest common denominator would have become the standard; many precision commands that could not be mapped to other systems would have been eliminated. In other words, power and flexibility would have been overridden in favor of commonality and uniformity.

But as online services realized a larger market share among less-skilled users, ease of use evolved into a pressing issue for them. Menu systems were the first steps services took toward making the systems more usable, with products such as Dialog's Knowledge Index and BRS's After Dark in the 1980s. Then, in the mid-1990s, many providers took it one step further, revamping their command systems into GUIs. The change in interface styles kicked off some fundamental trade-off issues associated with task support and usability.

In general, command interfaces—as a design style for any interface—give users more control over their tasks. But as this chapter has just discussed, there is a downside to command interfaces: Indisputably, command interfaces have a steep learning curve that deters most novice and intermediate end users. Command systems have a complex language structure that requires memorization if mastery is ever going to be achieved.[26] By comparison, GUIs are the friendlier of the two interface styles. A GUI is easier to navigate than a command interface for most users because graphical elements allow users to rely on recognition instead of total recall.[27] But a design trade-off is that GUIs can be slow and unyielding. Preordained pathways and pull-down menus mean the possibility for fewer shortcuts, leading to slower navigation and contributing to increases in users' frustration levels as they naturally improve. Table 6.2 (see page 154) provides a general overview of the comparative advantages of command interface styles.[28]

Interface style trade-offs outlined in Table 6.2 shed important light on the online service redesigns. What the GUI online service remakes have delivered is an interface that is more focused on *usability* than on the earlier goal of *task support*. Specifically, GUIs help users interact with systems by giving them the abilities to multitask in a Windows environment, to directly manipulate content and icons on the screen with a mouse and get immediate

---

Table 6.2 Trade-Offs Between Interface Styles: Command Versus GUI

	Advantages	Disadvantages
Command Interface	Flexibility, supports user initiative, supports macro capability	Requires substantial training and memorization, difficult to retain, poor error handling
Graphical User Interface (GUI)	Visually presents task, easy to learn, easy to retain, errors can be avoided, encourages exploration, high subjective satisfaction	May require graphics display/pointing devices, more programming effort until tools improve, may be hard to record history or write macros

Source: Ben Shneiderman, "A Taxonomy and Rule Base for Selection of Interface Styles," in Ronald Baecker, Jonathan Grudin, William S. Buxton, and Saul Greenberg, eds., *Readings in Human-Computer Interaction: Toward the Year 2000*, San Francisco: Morgan Kaufman Publishers, Inc., Second Edition, 1995, p. 401.

---

results, to intuitively navigate by pointing and clicking, and to visually receive feedback about activation and help. These are all interface traits that are particularly appealing to end users.

But whether each service's interface has actually taken full advantage of the design potential that GUIs afford is a whole different matter. Not long ago, I wrote an article comparing the GUI redesigns of DataTimes EyeQ and Dow Jones/News Retrieval.[29] In particular, I found that even though inherent design opportunities for usability existed with the GUI style, one system failed and the other succeeded. The design of EyeQ (when it was still a DataTimes product) left users feeling unempowered, offering little navigability between windows for multitasking, providing little consistency from screen to screen in layout and functions, and overloading the search screen with incomprehensible and poorly scaled icons. The net effect was a design that overwhelmed the end-user market that the service wanted to attract and frustrated the expert market the company had long served. By comparison, News/Retrieval took full advantage of the GUI potential for empowering users, communicating visually, and encouraging interaction. For example, the design of News/Retrieval included two interfaces (GUI and Command) that supported both sets of primary users, used a frames approach in layout that enhanced ease of use and multitasking; provided an optimal number of meaningful icons per page; and delivered a low-key design that helped users focus on their searching tasks and get help, if they needed it.

Aesthetics: Now for Something Completely Different

Undoubtedly, as this chapter shows, times have changed for the commercial online services. Nowhere is it more apparent than in each system's aesthetics. Creating a system with visual design is a huge departure for some providers. Dialog, for example, used to provide a question mark as their only design element on their original opening screen.

Because of their GUI transformations, Web databases require a full-blown design language with elements (icons, color, and functions), organizing principles, and qualifying principles that visually communicate to users and encourage interaction. An added constraint is that most Web databases are not starting off with a clean slate: They are reconfiguring a command language-style information retrieval interface into a GUI. In many cases, the aesthetics of Web database design show the effects of being a round peg forced into a square hole.

But these design challenges are far from new. Developers on the Xerox Star project grappled with many of these same problems when they tried to develop the world's first commercial GUI. (For more about the Star project, see chapter 3.) One of the key issues on the Star project was "creating

---

Table 6.3 GUI Graphic Principles from the Xerox Star Project

- Creating appropriate effect that captures all of the subjective and emotional impact that different graphics can convey

- A match with the medium so that there is a consistent quality in graphics that makes the most of the given medium

- A consistent graphical vocabulary throughout

- Visual order and user focus that draws users' attention to the most important features of the display

- The illusion of manipulable objects that are familiar to users and reduce learning time

- Revealed structure that shows up when users select functions

---

Source: William Verplank, "Graphic Challenges in Designing Object-Oriented User Interfaces," in M. Helander, ed. *Handbook of Human-Computer Interaction*, New York: North Holland, p. 366.

effective and appropriate graphics."[30] Six guiding graphic principles, which appear in Table 6.3, were generated to help guide the team's design efforts.[31]

Even though the guidelines are almost 20 years old, the principles in Table 6.3 have applicability for evaluators judging the effectiveness of Web databases. One area where Web databases have struggled is with matching the Web medium. Some Web databases could not be more at odds with what the Web is about if they tried. Many are closed, proprietary systems with an absence of any hypertext links (an obvious device for enhancing value-added content). Besides the opportunities, there are pitfalls to the Web medium, too, that Web databases unavoidably match. As Anne Mintz discusses in her interview, the Web simplifies what has always been easy about searching (checking off date limitations), which is a plus. But Web databases leave the complexity of formulating search queries to the users, as the systems always have.

So far, Web database design does little to support the complexities of information retrieval. The two cognitive activities, selecting and strategizing, are wildly different. Pulling down a menu and selecting a range of dates is a far less rigorous task than thinking out a search statement to type in a small empty dialog box. The tasks are cognitively incongruous—at odds with one another. It is no wonder that end users generally simplify search queries on the Web.

Design evaluation, as this book has argued, is a relatively new practice for many information professionals. Nevertheless, it is a design issue, the overall layout of Web databases, that is beginning to register discontent with power searchers. Work space on the Web makes users feel cramped, at best. As one power searcher points out about one Web database, the overhead of the browsers' navigational buttons, the systems' Web buttons, and the command boxes at the bottom only allow one citation to be viewed at a time.[32] Because of the limited screen, layout is a tricky beast. Available functions and features must be minimized and prioritized even more than in traditional GUI design for other products like CDs. A classic example has an opening screen with a lot of fanfare and graphics, but has a button, leading to a search function that is well "below the fold." Another one of Star's principles— ordering and focusing users' attention through the visuals of a design—is violated with this design choice.

A nagging problem with Web design, in general, is providing a consistent graphical vocabulary throughout a site. There is a dual burden for Web databases: They need to establish a look and feel to their site that carries throughout all of the pages, and they need to identify key functions early on—like log off, help, start over—and then offer them all consistently in the same place on each screen. The aspect of consistency is especially important for the services to uphold on the Web because users can become disoriented about which site they are on. Use of coordinated colors, fonts, headers, and typography, consistently applied throughout, can help create a unified graphical vocabulary that makes navigation and processing a lot easier for users. The GUI environment also fosters iconography. In theory, icons, small pictographs for conveying information, reduce users' needs for memorization. In effect, icons act like idioms. But using icons so that they add to users' ability to visually process information is problematic. For starters, icons often do not scale well. They can also be difficult to decipher, failing when they try to convey complex actions through a picture.

The Point

There is an idea advanced in HCI about designing for user cultures. One theory states that some online system design styles are more culturally fitting for certain sets of users than for others, based on their work settings and how the users regard their use of time.[33] Further, the authors make an important distinction between *internal versus external* systems.[34] In particular, they argue that systems that offer internal control are designed to give users full control over configuring and adapting a system to their own needs. These systems work particularly well for user cultures that value precision in their information retrieval tasks. By comparison, external systems are designed so that users can sit back and accept at face value the services the vendor provides. External systems are optimal for user cultures that like to be guided and to browse by example.[35] The theory makes sense: Some users want to have internal control over a system, while others prefer to accept the system as it is presented to them.

When it comes to online commercial systems and their remakes, the idea of designing for user cultures is telling. What has happened as design has changed from command systems to Web databases is that support for one culture has been substituted with support for another. In other words, the old command systems that supported control and precision are giving way to a new design regime that supports guidance. Interestingly enough, many old-time users have registered a feeling of culture shock with the changes in interface styles. In light of this theory, it comes as no surprise. In order for Web databases to survive as powerful information retrieval tools, the providers' biggest challenge will be to develop systems that support the cultural diversity of the end-user groups they are trying to attract, while developing systems that preserve the power-searching culture they have long supported. A compilation of design evaluation criteria for Web databases appears in Table 6.4.[36]

Table 6.4 *Online Commercial Database Design Evaluation Checklist*

• Users are presented with at least two interfaces, simple and advanced, insuring flexibility for users' skill levels (beginning versus intermediate versus advanced) and how their skill levels may change over time.

• The interfaces support command line and GUI searches, ensuring the flexibility for users' skill levels and the kinds of tasks they need to complete (simple searching versus precision searching).

• Log-in occurs at the beginning of the program, long before searching ever begins so that users' concentration on search tasks is uninterrupted.

• Web databases offer the same search and field options that their command predecessors did so that power searching is not compromised and the remakes are not underpowered. In particular, Web databases need to support multiple database searching, iterative searching, and command stacking.

• Visuals help users focus on the tasks they are most likely to use on a regular basis. Start and search buttons are prominently displayed "above the fold" on opening pages.

• Search capabilities are integrated into underlying data so that users have full control over manipulating database content and so that consistency is built into it.

• Thesauri and indexing help link related data so that more intelligence is built into the system, and searching by natural language is supported.

• Simple and advanced search examples are provided on Web databases so users can learn how to fully take advantage of the system instead of reverting to simplified searching methods.

- Web databases and GUIs use consistent graphical vocabulary and meaningful icons so that what is learned on one screen can be applied throughout the system.

- The status of processing is relayed via menu bars and through feedback boxes, showing the number of records being found, so that users know the system is working.

- Forgiveness is worked into Web database and GUIs—users can reverse their actions quickly with back buttons and bulletin boxes.

- Web databases offer users direct manipulation that delivers quick results so that users remain engaged.

- Result screens provide users with enough information—title, author, type of document, length, and summary information—so that users can make effective decisions before selecting documents.

- Outputting selected records on Web databases is direct, intuitive, and requires few steps. Users are not required to save to their caches.

- The Windows environment supports multitasking within the program and with other software packages on the hard drive.

- Web databases have a simple, straightforward design, especially a layout that allows room for the browser, the system's own navigational bar, and results without overwhelming and distracting users.

- Color is consistently applied so that users subliminally register that they are within the same system as they move from screen to screen.

Table 6.5 The Pick of the Lot: Recommended Readings and Web Sites

Mary Ellen Bates, "Knight-Ridder on the Web: A Brave New World for Searchers?" *Searcher*, vol. 5, no. 6, June 1997, pp. 28–37.

Lloyd Alan Fletcher, "The Battle for the End User: Business Information Comes to the Desktop," *Searcher*, vol. 3, no. 8, Sept. 1995, pp. 32–40.

Alison J. Head, "A Question of Interface Design: How Do Online Service GUIs Measure Up?" *ONLINE*, vol. 21, no. 3, May/June 1997, pp. 20–9. Also available http://www.onlineinc.com/onlinemag/MayOL97/head5.html.

Ben Shneiderman, "A Taxonomy and Rule Base for Selection of Interface Styles," In Ronald Baecker, Jonathan Grudin, William S. Buxton, and Saul Greenberg, eds. *Readings in Human-Computer Interaction: Toward the Year 2000*, San Francisco: Morgan Kaufman Publishers, Inc., 2nd ed., 1995, pp. 401–9.

INSIDE . . .

An Interview with Anne Mintz about Searching Online Commercial Databases

Anne Mintz is Director of Information Services for Forbes Inc. and a well-known information industry author and conference panelist. She has been an online searcher since 1974.

What makes you a power searcher? How does your approach to online information retrieval differ from a typical end user's approach?

Power searchers spend a lot of time looking for answers in electronic services and other places and have been doing so for a long time. As a power searcher, I *think* differently than people who do not have my training in information science. My thinking is more lateral because I am a generalist. Also, I think in terms of the old-line reference question and interview, in which you try to get the person who asked you the question to tell you exactly what it is that they are looking for and not what they have told you they are looking for. As a power searcher, I'm doing research for someone else and I have a critic in the end user that has asked me the question.

End users don't have that. They just have themselves. They either find what they think is the answer or they think they have found enough when, in fact, they may have found very little. I have somebody who is going to tell me that this is or it isn't what they are looking for. Power searchers use resources to do things that they weren't intended to do. For example, when the Who's Who directories went up on Dialog, most people used them to find people. A power searcher looks at this source and immediately thinks, I can look up and find people who list themselves as members of the University Club! Finally, I think about value in terms of not just the money that is invested but in terms of the time that is invested in using a source. And I don't think end users think that way. They think more in terms of money, how much the search costs.

What are commercial online services especially good at when it comes to professional research?

I can name two completely different things. One of them is the categorizing and the tagging of fields. Even Nexis, which really deals in natural language and text, indexes to a certain degree. Indexing allows for segment searching so that you can search a part of an article whether it's a headline, byline, the text itself, the captions, or the graphics. Services that do that in the commercial realm are adding value that you don't get, particularly on the Internet, or even when newspapers or magazines put their text up on the Web in an archive. Services give you controlled field searching that is very useful, especially when it is consistent. A provider that has thought this through in his or her programming will understand that you don't want every article that appears on Microsoft or Bill Gates. So some services will allow you to search just the headlines or lead paragraphs or captions fields. The other thing that online services are good at is collecting money. On the Web, you have to use a credit card or you have to do a whole lot of other stuff, where an online service is very good at billing you and telling you what you have been billed for.

What are the most difficult reference questions to answer using online services?

Concepts. Trends. Here's one: "It looks to me like stiletto heels are coming back, is that true?" The problem is that what you are looking for is natural language and the way people describe things. Those shoes were called spike heels and high heels, too. As a searcher, you have to use a lot of synonyms to get at your concept. It is very hard to query a system and ask, "Is there a trend in . . . ?" That's not the way things are written. *Forbes* is written in a very different style than *Vanity Fair* and for an entirely different audience. You wouldn't expect an article on the same topic in these publications to use the same natural language.

How have GUI remakes and Web interactivity affected your own interaction with the systems?

The Web has completely standardized all of the features that we worked so hard for years to get from vendors; some have even gone away. Iterative searching is an example of this. That means you ask ten questions, you have ten different sets of questions that get saved, and you can go back and combine them. On a lot of systems on the Web, that went away. The Web, at large, does not encourage that kind of structure. The Web encourages, "Ask a question, get an answer." Specifically, Web databases do not allow you to mix and match your results. The Web allows providers to *make* simple that which *is* simple. What I mean by that is that some commercial services have said, "Okay, point and click at the dates you want to cover, then point and click at the publications that you want this search to include." This takes away the complexity of data limitation and combining sources, allowing what could have been simple all along to be simple in a visual way. Web database design cleans up that part, it's a positive attribute, leaving only the search queries. Web search queries are not ready to take the Boolean power from command interfaces and transfer it over. The problem is that Web databases have presumed a simplicity to research that does not exist. The Web is easy, but the research stays hard.

What are the limitations of Web databases, in general?

What happens if your network goes down or Bell Atlantic cuts off your T1 line or you can't get on the Web? Your computer dies. A flood takes out your electricity for two days. What do you do? The answer for me is that I have to have a library collection where I keep CD-ROMs and print sources that I would not normally keep as a librarian. We are extremely dependent on the computer and on the phone. You need back-up, redundancy in your collection of sources. Also, the Web doesn't have everything, by far. Sometimes people want to see the image or a table in a newspaper story. I turn to the microfilm.

Endnotes

1. Trudi Bellardo Hahn, "Pioneers of the Online Age," *Information Processing and Management*, vol. 32, no. 1, 1996, p. 39.
2. Hahn, op. cit., p. 45.
3. There are, of course, the horror stories of exorbitant bills when new searchers have forgotten to log-off and there is even one case of a vendor's redesign, which failed to provide an automatic log-off to the surprise of many users. The vendor was DataTimes as relayed by Lloyd Alan Fletcher in "The Battle for the End User: Business Information Comes to the Desktop," *Searcher*, vol. 3, no. 8, September 1995, pp. 32–40.
4. John Marcus, "Mining for Full-Text Gold on a Deadline: Information Technology Subject Coverage on the Three Major Services," *DATABASE*, vol. 18, no. 2, April/May 1995. Provides one of the most current and thorough product reviews of Lexis, Dow Jones News/Retrieval, and Dialog.
5. Marcus, op. cit., p. 84.
6. John Rosenberg, "Road Testing LEXIS-NEXIS' New Search Aid Software," *Searcher*, vol. 5, no. 4, July/Aug. 1997, pp. 48–58.
7. The Profound system was the first major online system to offer Web interactivity, according to Mick O'Leary, "The Business Information Services: Old Line Moves to the Web," *Computers in Libraries*, vol. 17, no. 6, June 1997, p. 31.

8. Barbara Quint from the periodical *Information Today*, May 1996 as the quote appeared in Amelia Kassel, "Here They Come!: Database Producers on the Web," *Searcher*, vol. 5, no. 7, July/August 1997, p. 26.

9. Mary Ellen Bates in "Knight-Ridder on the Web: A Brave New World for Searchers?" *Searcher*, vol. 5, no. 6, June 1997, p. 28. Bates writes that Knight Ridder Information, Inc., formerly Dialog, had to rehire back retired programmers, on a temporary basis, to fix ailing mainframe systems and carry out upgrades.

10. Fletcher, op. cit., p. 33, quotes Allen Paschal, then president and CEO of DataTimes, now with The Gale Group.

11. Fletcher, op. cit., p. 35.

12. Ibid.

13. Leonard Fuld as quoted in Kassel, op. cit., p. 27.

14. Ibid.

15. Kassel, op. cit., p. 35. Wording and explanation are slightly modified for use in this chapter.

16. Bates, op. cit., p. 37.

17. Bates, op. cit. p. 31.

18. Kassel, op. cit. p. 28.

19. Bates, op. cit., p. 31.

20. Ibid.

21. Fletcher, op. cit., pp. 32–48.

22. Marcus, op. cit., p. 85.

23. Hahn, op. cit., p. 34.

24. Albert Krichmar, "Command Language Ease of Use: A Comparison of Dialog and Orbit," *ONLINE Review*, vol. 5, no. 3, 1981, p. 227–40.

25. Ibid. See also Marcus, op. cit., pp. 81–5.

26. Krichmar, op. cit., p. 228.

27. Alison J. Head, "A Question of Interface Design: How Do Online Service GUIs Measure Up?" *ONLINE*, vol. 21, no. 3, May/June 1997, p. 28.

28. Ben Shneiderman, "A Taxonomy and Rule Base for Selection of Interface Styles," in Ronald Baecker, Jonathan Grudin, William S. Buxton, and Saul Greenberg, eds., *Readings in Human-Computer Interaction: Toward the Year 2000*, San Francisco: Morgan Kaufman Publishers, Inc., Second Edition, 1995, p. 401.

29. Head, op. cit., pp. 20–9. GUI versions (not Web databases) of Dow Jones News/Retrieval 5.0 and DataTimes EyeQ 1.22 were tested in January/February 1997.

30. William Verplank, "Graphic Challenges in Designing Object-Oriented User Interfaces." In M. Helander, ed., *Handbook of Human-Computer Interaction*, New York: North Holland, 1988, pp. 365–76.

31. Verplank, op. cit., p. 366. Table 6.3 has slightly modified wording and added explanation for use in this chapter.

32. Bates, op. cit., p. 32.

33. Peter Wooliams and David Gee, "Accounting for User Diversity in Configuring Online Systems," *ONLINE Review*, vol. 16, no. 5, 1992, pp. 303–11.

34. Ibid.

35. Wooliams and Gee, op. cit., p. 309.

36. This checklist is a compilation, which was drawn from my own research and thoughts about the design of online commercial databases and from the evaluation checklists and comments developed in Bates, op. cit., pp. 28-37; Marcus, op. cit., pp. 81–5; Head, op. cit., pp. 20-9; Verplank, op. cit., pp. 365-76; and Kassel, op. cit., pp. 26–35.

7 Four Predictions

The last chapter of *Design Wise* is a departure from the rest of the book. These pages do not address the design of existing information resources, but the future of them. What appears here are four educated guesses about what will happen to information resources and the people who work with them. The sources of these predictions are based on many of the emerging trends identified throughout this book.

Prediction One: Take the Money and Run

In the next two years, new players will enter the information resource business arena with a vengeance, shaking up things for traditional information providers. History will repeat itself but not entirely in the same way. Just as the mainstay provider, Dialog, came from the unlikely origins of Lockheed Missile and Space Company in the 1960s and 1970s, companies with seemingly distant ties to the business of selling content will emerge as key players. The difference is that this time there will be an influx of niche information resources. A growing management initiative called knowledge management (KM) is setting the stage. This is how:

In layperson's terms, KM is about capturing workers' intellectual capital, which is usually tacit, and distributing it with new technologies (e.g.,

167

intranets). The end goal of most KM projects is to strengthen a company's innovative and competitive stance through widespread knowledge sharing. So far, most companies are at a stage of discovering how to get the most from the knowledge management process, experimenting with intranets and creating information repositories for information sharing that draw from knowledge that workers keep in their heads or have filed away with other print-only documents.

But once companies get an accounting of their knowledge capital, some of the more entrepreneurial ones will discover they also have digitized knowledge commodities, unbeknownst to them before, that have market value. Some companies will decide to pick and choose from their knowledge stockpile, holding back information with competitive advantage, but selling off other information resources on the open market. The beauty of the deal is that many companies will already have developed an interface that is in place, and most likely runs on a Web platform.

How might this transformation actually happen? Here is a hypothetical case. A Web site development company discovers that they have information about their niche market (e.g., the consumer habits of 30- to 40-year-olds based on ten years of studies, observations, and sales) and loads the best of the information on an intranet, which has been designed in-house for knowledge sharing. This information may have tremendous marketing value for other businesses that may not be direct competitors but have an interest in this age group. The company decides to test the commercial waters and lowers its intranet's firewalls to paying parties. Users flock to the source, partially out of the content's exclusivity and value and partially out of the resource's accessibility. The Web development company has developed a marketable niche product no one else has.

There are two components—an awareness of information as a salable commodity and the Web as a ubiquitous delivery system—that make these kinds of niche information resources a possibility. Niche products will inevitably be bundled into larger KM megadatabase projects once standard protocols for sharing information are in place. Other players besides commercial companies will play an increasingly important role, too. An emerging example of this is the Instructional Management Systems (IMS) project sponsored by EDUCAUSE, a national consortium of private sector businesses and educational institutions. As part of the EDUCAUSE National Learning Infrastructure Initiative (NLII), IMS is laying an important information technology foundation by working to create a suite of standard protocols for sharing widely dispersed training information.

Prediction Two: Intelligent Agents Will Fall Short of the Hype . . .

The promise of intelligent agents will be the letdown of the computing field's promises. By intelligent agents, I do not mean the simple intermediary types of agents who take care of something that someone else would have had to do, such as automatically resetting the clock on your screen when daylight saving time occurs. I mean a more advanced agent—the soft robot—highly anticipated in computer circles since the 1950s. As envisioned, intelligent agents would take their marching orders from users, go out and monitor the information spaces, interact with other intelligent agents and swap information, and then retrieve anything they think users may want or need over time. The results would then be presented to computer users in a highly customized way that does not overload individual cognitive sensibilities. When it comes to information retrieval, the ideal intelligent agent is basically a "reference librarian in a box."

Some of the most enduring hype about the promise of intelligent agents was stirred up by Apple's promotional and futuristic video, *The Knowledge Navigator*, which was released in 1988. In the video's story, a harried university professor has the help of "Phil," an intelligent agent who is a nattily dressed man on the computer screen, solving everything from locating newly published research for the professor's next lecture to instantly updating maps and dropping them into a multimedia presentation program—all in matter of seconds. But even if the Apple video is darned entertaining, and even if competitors like Microsoft have poured hundreds of thousands of dollars into developing intelligent agents that don't come close to Phil, the dream will not be realized in the next ten years, if ever. Customizable agents that filter through scads of unruly content and then deliver back to users just what they want are about as plausible as daffodil blooms in December.

Here are a few reasons why. So far, as we have seen throughout this book, information systems have faced great difficulty dealing with capturing the nuances of human behavior involving information retrieval. To put it bluntly, intelligent agent design is an advanced course in information retrieval, far beyond the form-filling search interfaces and search engines that are currently on the Web. As Lou Rosenfeld points out in chapter 5, searching for known items on the Web is easy; however, beyond that, the abstractness of searching or browsing for information that users cannot quite describe becomes an automation world that is far from being conquered. So far, agents have done well in interpreting a bit stream of data. But beyond a linear feed, agents run into trouble. The problems will compound as the Web undoubtedly moves toward more and more multimedia and agents fall further and further behind as they try to process users' natural language requests for non-linear and converged sources, beginning with images.

Another problem that librarians have long recognized is that users' information needs are anything but static, consistent, and/or context-free. Predictably, users want different kinds of information at various times. Also, users get smarter and, at times, dumber (forgetting different things they once knew). Agents that can interact with users and play a sophisticated host to their highly volatile information needs are a wonderful idea, but do not look for agents to deliver true filtering in the next ten years. Even if most of the technological hurdles could be cleared, Pattie Maes of the MIT Media Laboratory has identified two further challenges for agent design: (1) ongoing agent competence and (2) gaining users' trust so that tasks are freely delegated to agents.[1]

Prediction Three: . . . But Searching Will Become More Intelligent

Even though advanced intelligent agents will fall short of many industry expectations, search interfaces will become more intelligent. As Web content grows, the inadequacies of search engines will only continue to mount, stretching users' patience with every turn. Within a year or two, a new type of search engine will provide users with more options for controlling what they input and what they get back. Mechanisms, such as the eXtensible Markup Language (XML) and the Resource Description Framework (RDF) from the World Wide Web Consortium, are setting the stage for this kind of development. In particular, XML has generated a lot of excitement because it gives designers a tagging system that can make their Web content far more informative. XML provides relatively sophisticated ways to add structured markup to Web documents, making networked information discovery and retrieval more precise and effective. In layperson's terms, XML has been compared to being like an envelope around a letter.[2] Even though the real information may be the letter (or Web page), by reading the envelope (or accessing tagged information), users gather contextual information that has value, such as where the letter (Web page) was sent from, when, by whom, and other information that *profiles* what is contained in the package.

I have dubbed this type of improved search interface—*partnerware*—because of the interface's collaboration with users and their tasks. The ideal model for partnerware would have two important features: (1) the ability to recognize and recall users' previous search behavior and (2) the ability to customize what users get back from a search based on users' preferences. The first feature that recalls search behavior would give users the option of calling up previous search queries and strategies. For ongoing research, this feature could be a real time-saver. So far, Web development has done little to remember users and their preferences. When users go to the current search engine, they must begin with a blank slate. The Web treats every user's request as spontaneous, original—virginal. So far, search engine design is not capable of recalling what users have looked for before or what terms may have been used before. (At best, the browser allows users to bookmark sites that they may plan on revisiting.) The interface design puts most of the work on users, offering few customizing features for research work. Partnerware could share the work that users need to do each time they perform a search.

The second feature of partnerware would give users the ability to customize their search results before they ever see them. So far, XML holds the promise as a key, if you believe the computer press and conference proceedings. The advantage for users would be that they could gain control over the information deluge of the Web. There could be a built-in method in the interface for users to eliminate the kinds of content in which they have no interest. For example, if the user wants to see only sites with the "edu" domain, authored in the past six months, and with a full bibliography, partnerware would deliver only those results that match the criteria. In effect, partnerware does most of the sorting tasks, instead of the user.

Prediction Four: Information Professionals Take a Leap Backwards

Information professionals, librarians, cybrarians (whatever title you prefer) will be employable far into the future in emerging roles that take them far beyond information provision. As more and more information is democratized and put into end users' hands, information professionals will play a vital role not only in selecting online information resources but in designing information resources. Even though the technology and delivery systems may be different, information professionals will be returning to one of the profession's oldest foundations: toolmaking.[3] Just as they did with their development of the Dewey Decimal and Library of Congress classification systems, information professionals will play an important information management and design role with Web development. In a few cases, information professionals have already begun, sitting on teams with programmers and developers who are building and designing systems for a given use. This trend will continue.

Information professionals will contribute and accelerate an important dimension to user-centered design, especially through their understanding of information-seeking behavior or "which kinds of people seek which kinds of information through which channels."[4] As Anne Mintz so aptly points out in chapter 6, power searchers are different creatures from end users. End users want quick answers from systems; they care little about which fields are available and how they might be applied. Researchers, by contrast, are fascinated by the inner workings of information systems and how users interact with them. In the design and development of information resources, information professionals will bring a much-needed piece to the puzzle. The systems they work to create will have three defining characteristics: (1) support for the different search behaviors every user exhibits; (2) rigorous underlying indexing and thesauri classification systems that put users in touch with what they are seeking; and (3) methods that creatively help users develop search queries and strategies on their own.

Endnotes

1. Pattie Maes, "Agents that Reduce Work and Information Overload," *Communications of the ACM*, vol. 37, no. 7, July 1994, pp. 31–40.
2. Brian Travis is cited for the comparison in "XML Packages Data Like an Envelope," *Web 98 Conference*, September 23, 1998. Available http://webreview.com/wr/pub/web98east/23/xmlday2.html. 21 Feb. 1999.

3. Thanks to Stuart Sutton, Associate Professor, School of Information, Syracuse University who first described information professionals as toolmakers to his audience during his June 1994 Special Libraries' Association Conference presentation in Atlanta, Georgia. Later these ideas were formally published as Stuart A. Sutton, "Core Competencies for the Information Professions and the Evolution of Skills Sets," *Education Libraries*, vol. 18, no. 3, pp. 6–11.

4. E. Parker and W. J. Paisley, *Patterns of Information Seeking*, Palo Alto, Calif.: Stanford University Press, 1966.

Bibliography

ACM/SIGCHI Curricula for Human-Computer Interaction, p. 16, © 1992, ACM. Figure 1.1 is used by permission from the Association for Computing Machinery.

Alliance for Technology Access's *Computer Resources for People with Disabilities*. Alameda, Calif.: Hunter House, 1996.

Americans with Disabilities Act (ADA) home page. Available http://www.usdoj.gov/crt/ada. 21 Feb. 1999.

"Amazon.com Seeks to Triple Shares." *San Jose Mercury News*, April 19, 1998, p. E16.

Baecker, Ronald, Jonathan Grudin, William S. Buxton, and Saul Greenberg, eds. *Readings in Human-Computer Interaction: Toward the Year 2000*. San Francisco: Morgan Kaufman Publishers, Inc., 2nd ed., 1995.

Basch, Reva. *Researching Online for Dummies*. Foster City, Calif.: IDG Press, 1998.

———. *Secrets of the Super Net Searchers*. Medford, N.J.: Information Today, Inc., 1966.

Bates, Marcia. "Where Should the Person Stop and the Information Search Interface Start?" *Information Processing and Management*, vol. 26, no. 5, 1990, pp. 575–91.

Bates, Mary Ellen. "Knight-Ridder on the Web: A Brave New World for Searchers?" *Searcher*, vol. 5, no. 6, June 1997, pp. 28–37.

Bergman, Eric, and Earl Johnson. "Designing for Accessibility." Sun Microsystems' Technology and Research Page. Available http://www.sun.com/tech.access/. 21 Feb. 1999.

———. "Towards Accessible Human-Computer Interaction." Available on Sun's Technology and Research site at: http://www.sun.com/tech/access/ updt.HCI.advance.html. 21 Feb. 1999.

Berkman, Jerry. "Web Design and Maintenance." *ACM SIGUCCS XXV*, New York: Association for Computing Machinery, 1997, pp. 23–7.

Borges, Jose, Israel Morales, and Nestor J. Rodriguez. "Guidelines for Designing Usable World Wide Web Pages." *CHI 96 Conference*, New York: Association for Computing Machinery, ACM Press 1996, pp. 277–8.

Bortman, Henry. "What's Your DQ?" *MacUser*, July 1997, p. 21.

Bosch, Stephen, Patricia Promis, and Chris Sugnet. *Guide to Selecting and Acquiring CD-ROMs, Software and Other Electronic Publications.* Chicago: American Library Association, 1994.

Bosch, Victoria Manglano, and Micheline Hancock-Beaulieu. "CDROM User Interface Evaluation: The Appropriateness of GUIs." *Online & CD ROM Review*, vol. 19, no. 5, 1995, pp. 255–70.

Brennan, Susan. "Conversation as Direct Manipulation: An Iconoclastic View." In Brenda Laurel, ed., *The Art of Human-Computer Interface Design*, Reading, Mass.: Addison-Wesley, 1990, pp. 393–404.

Buel, Stephen. "Business Leap Ahead on Net: The Trend Could Boost Economy and Reshape Some US Industries." *San Jose Mercury News*, April 16, 1998, p. 1A.

Burg, Barbara. "Virtual Knowledge: The Best Buys in 1998 CD-ROM Encyclopedias." *Searcher*, vol. 6, no. 4, April 1998, pp. 57–63.

Burgstahler, Sheryl, Dan Comden, and Beth Fraser. "Universal Access: Designing and Evaluating Web Sites for Accessibility." *CHOICE*, v. 34, Supplement 1997, pp. 19–22.

Callaway, Erin. "The Web Is a Different World for GUI Design." *PC Week*, November 13, 1995, v. 12, n. 45, p. 26.

Card, Stuart, Thomas Moran, and Allen Newell. *The Psychology of Human-Computer Interaction.* Hillsdale, N.J.: Lawrence Erlbaum Associates, 1983.

Carvajal, Donna. "Online Bookstores Do Battle." *New York Times* article as it appeared in *The Santa Rosa Press Democrat* on March 17, 1998, p. E1.

Caywood, Carolyn. "Library Selection Criteria for WWW Resources." Available http://www6.pilot.infi.net/~carolyn/criteria.html. May 1998.

Christierson, Eric, and Donna Pontau. "Universal Design for Library Web Pages: Providing Access for Users with Disabilities," *San Jose State University Faculty Diversity Grant Project: 1998.* Available http://www.drc.sjsu.edu. 21 Feb. 1999.

Cooper, Alan. *About Face: The Essentials of User Interface Design.* Foster City, Calif.: IDG Books Worldwide, Inc., 1995.

Cottrell, Janet, and Michael B. Eisenberg. "Web Design for Information Problem-Solving: Maximizing Value for Users." *Computers in Libraries*, vol. 17, no. 5, May 1997, pp. 52–7.

Crow, Raymond W., and Robert F. Starbird. "Easier Said than Done: Practical Considerations in User Interface Design." *Government Information Quarterly*, vol. 9, no. 2, 1992, pp. 169–85.

Deines-Jones, Courtney. "EASI Access to Library Technology." *Library Hi Tech News*, June 1997, pp. 18–31.

Desmarais, Norman. *The Librarian's CD-ROM Handbook.* Westport, Conn.: Meckler, 1989.

Dix, Alan, Jayne Finlay, Gregory Abowd, and Russell Beale. *Human-Computer Interaction.* Englewood Cliffs, N.J.: Prentice-Hall, 1993.

Dumas, Joseph. *Designing User Interface Software.* Englewood Cliffs, N.J.: Prentice-Hall, 1988.

Ehrlich, Kate. "So You Wanna Design for the Web." *interactions* (ACM journal), March 1996, pp. 19–23.

Einstein, David. "Encyclopedia Evolution: They've Been Transformed to Interactive Tools." *San Francisco Chronicle*, February 3, 1998, p. C3.

Elkind, J. "The Incidences of Disabilities in the United States." *Human Factors*, vol. 32, no. 4, 1990, pp. 397–405.

Elshami, Ahmed M. *CD-ROM Technology for Information Managers.* Chicago: American Library Association, 1990.

Fidler, Roger. *Mediamorphosis.* Thousand Oaks, Calif.: Pine Forge Press, 1997.

Finlay, M. ed. *Facts and Figures 1993: CD-ROM and Multimedia CDs.* London: TFPL Publishing, 1993.

Fletcher, Lloyd Alan. "The Battle for the End User: Business Information Comes to the Desktop." *Searcher*, vol. 3, no. 8, Sept. 1995, pp. 32–48.

Fleming, Jennifer. "In Defense of Web Graphics: Graphic Designers Offer More Than Just Flashy Graphics." *Web Review*, July 25, 1997. Available http://webreview.comwr/pub/97/07/25/feature/index4.html. 21 Feb. 1999.

Forsythe, Chris, Eric Grose, and Julie Ratner, eds. *Human Factors and Web Development.* Mahwah, N.J.: Lawrence Erlbaum Associates, 1998.

Fuccella, Jeanette. "Using User Centered Design Methods to Create and Design Usable Web Sites." *SIGDOC 97 Snowbird*, New York: Association for Computing Machinery, ACM Press, 1997, pp. 69–77.

Garlick, Kristen L. *Building the Service-Based Library Web Site: A Step-by-Step Guide to Design and Options.* Chicago: American Library Association, 1996.

Gaver, William. "Technology Affordances." *CHI 91 Conference Proceedings*, Association for Computing Machinery, ACM Press, 1991 pp. 79–84.

Gould, John D. "How to Design Usable Systems." In Ronald Baecker, Jonathan Grudin, William S. Buxton, and Saul Greenberg, eds. *Readings in Human-Computer Interaction: Toward the Year 2000*. San Francisco: Morgan Kaufman Publishers, Inc., 2nd ed., 1995, pp. 93–121.

Grose Eric, Chris Forsythe, and Julie Ratner. "Using Interfaces and Traditional Style Guides to Design Interfaces." In Chris Forsythe, Eric Grose, and Julie Ratner, eds., *Human Factors and Web Development*, Mahwah, N.J.: Lawrence Erlbaum Publishers, 1998, pp. 121–36.

Grudin, Jonathan. "The Case Against User Consistency." *Communications of the ACM*, vol. 32, no. 10, Oct. 1989, pp. 1164–73.

Hahn, Trudi Bellardo. "Pioneers of the Online Age." *Information Processing & Management*, vol. 32, no. 1, 1996, pp. 33–48.

Harry, Veronica, and Charles Oppenheim. "Evaluations of Electronic Databases, Part 1: Criteria for Testing CD-ROM Products." *Online and CDROM Review*, vol. 17, no. 4, 1993, pp. 211–22.

Head, Alison J. "A Question of Interface Design: How Do Online Service GUIs Measure Up?" *ONLINE*, vol. 21, no. 3, May/June 1997, pp. 20-9. Also available http://www.onlineinc.com/onlinemag/mayol97/head5.html. 21 Feb. 1999.

———. "By Design: Are Microsoft's Animated Interface Agents Helpful," *ONLINE*, vol. 22, no. 1, Jan./Feb. 1998, pp. 19–28.

———. "Web Usability and Essential Design Issues." *Proceedings of National Online Meeting*, New York, May 1997, pp. 157–63.

Hewett, T., and R. Baecker, S. Card, T. Carey, J. Gasen, M. Mantiel, G. Perlman, G. Strong, and W. Verplank, "ACM SIGCHI Curricula for Human-Computer Interaction," *Report of the ACM SIGCHI Curriculum Development Group*, New York: Association for Computing Machinery, 1992, p. 5.

Horton, William, et al., *The Web Design Cookbook: All the Ingredients You Need to Create 5-Star Web Pages*. New York: Wiley, 1996.

Hutchins, E., J. Hollan, and D. Norman. "Direct Manipulation Interfaces." In Norman and Draper, eds., *User Centered Systems Design*, Mahwah, N.J.: Lawrence Erlbaum Publishers, 1986, pp. 87–124.

Hymes, Charles M., and Gary M. Olson. "Quick But Not So Dirty Web Design: Applying Empirical Conceptual Clustering Techniques to Organize Hypertext Content." *DIS '97 Amsterdam*, New York: Association for Computing Machinery, ACM Press, 1997, pp. 159–62.

"IntelliSense in Microsoft 97," *Microsoft White Paper*, Jan. 1997, pp. 1–13.

Jacsó, Péter. *CD-ROM Software, Dataware, and Hardware: Evaluation, Selection, and Installation*. Englewood, Colo.: Libraries Unlimited, 1992.

———. "Multimedia Strategies in Online Encyclopedias (Part One). *Information Today*, vol. 15, no. 4, April 1998, pp. 40–1.

———. "New Bottles?: The Currency of Databases." *ONLINE*, vol. 21, no. 2, March/April 1997, pp. 69–72.

———. "OVID Online: Puts on a Graphical (Inter) Face." *ONLINE*, vol., 20, no. 1, Jan./Feb. 1996, pp. 40–7.

Johnson, Chris. "The Ten Golden Rules for Providing Video Over the Web or 0% of 2.4M (at 270k/sec, 340 sec Remaining)." In Chris Forsythe, Eric Grose, and Julie Ratner, eds., *Human Factors and Web Development*. Mahwah, N.J.: Lawrence Erlbaum Publishers, 1998, pp. 207–21.

Johnson, Jeff, Terry Roberts, William Verplank, David C. Smith, Charles Irby, and Kevin Mackey. "Xerox Star: A Retrospective." *IEEE Computer*, vol. 22, no. 9, Sept. 1989, pp. 11–9.

Johnson. Steven. *Interface Culture: How New Technology Transforms the Way We Create and Communicate*. San Francisco: Harper Edge, 1997.

Kahn, Paul. "Visual Clues for Local and Global Coherence in the WWW." *Communications of the ACM*, vol. 38, no. 8, August 1995, pp. 67–9.

Kanerva, Amy, Kevin Keeker, Kirsten Risden, Eric Schuh, and Mary Czerwinski. "Web Usability Research at Microsoft Corporation." In Chris Forsythe, Eric Grose, and Julie Ratner, eds., *Human Factors and Web Development*, Mahwah, N.J.: Lawrence Erlbaum Publishers, 1998, pp. 189–98.

Kanter, Laurie, and Stephanie Rosenbaum. "Usability Studies of WWW Sites: Heuristic Evaluation vs. Laboratory Testing." *SIGDOC 97*, Snowbird, Utah, ACM Conference Proceedings, New York: Assocation for Computing Machinery, 1997, pp. 153–160.

Kapor, Mitchell. "A Software Design Manifesto" (speech originally delivered in 1990). Reprinted in Terry Winograd with John Bennett, Laura DeYoung, and Bradley Hartfield, eds., *Bringing Design to Software*. Reading, Mass.: Addison-Wesley Publishing Company, 1996, pp. 2–9.

Kassel, Amelia. "Here They Come!: Database Producers on the Web." *Searcher*, vol. 5, no. 7, July/Aug. 1997, pp. 26–35.

Kautzman, Amy K. "Virtuous, Virtual Access: Making Web Pages Accessible to People with Disabilities." *Searcher*, June 1998, pp. 42–7.

Kay, Alan. "User Interface: A Personal View." In Brenda Laurel, ed. *The Art of Human-Computer Interface Design*. Reading, Mass.: Addison-Wesley Publishing Company, 1990, pp. 191–207.

Kirkwood, Hal P. Jr. "Beyond Evaluation: A Model for Cooperative Evaluation of Internet Resources." *ONLINE*, vol. 22, no. 4, July-August, 1998, pp. 66–72.

Koczkodaj, Waldemar W., Marian Orlowski, Leila Wallenius, and Robert M. Wilson. "A Note on Using a Consistency-Driven Approach to CD-ROM Selection." *Library Software Review*, vol. 16., no. 1, Spring 1997, pp. 4–11.

Krichmar, Albert. "Command Language Ease of Use: A Comparison of DIALOG and ORBIT." *ONLINE Review*, vol. 5, no. 3, May/June 1981, pp. 227–40.

Lancaster, F. W., et al. "Searching Databases on CD-ROM: Comparison of the Results of End-User Searching with Results for Two Modes Searching by Skilled Intermediaries." *Reference Quarterly*, 1994, vol. 33, no. 3, pp. 370–86.

Lazzaro, Joseph. "Designing for a Wider Universe," *Web Review*, Sept. 4, 1998. Available http://webreview.com/wr/pub/98/09/04/feature/index2/html. 21 Feb. 1999.

Large, Andy. "The User Interface to CD-ROM Databases." *Journal of Librarianship and Information Science*, vol. 23, no. 4, Dec. 1991, pp. 203–217.

Laurel, Brenda, ed. *The Art of Human-Computer Interface Design*. Reading, Mass.: Addison-Wesley Publishing Company, 1990, pp. 269–78.

Leonard, Andrew. "Tough Room for the 'Toons.'" *Salon Magazine*, May 21, 1997. Available http://www.salonmagazine.com/may97/21st/articleb970501.html. 21 Feb. 1999.

Liddle, David. "Design of the Conceptual Model." In Terry Winograd, John Bennett, Laura DeYoung, and Bradley Hartfield, eds. *Bringing Design to Software*. Reading, Mass.: Addison-Wesley Publishing Company, 1996, pp. 18–36.

Lynch, Patrick J., and Sarah Horton. "Designing Reference Sites for the Web." Yale, C/AIM WWW Style Guide. Available http://www.info.med.yale.edu/caim/manual/contents.html. 21 Feb. 1999.

Maes, Pattie. "Agents that Reduce Work and Information Overload," *Communications of the ACM*, July 1994, vol. 37, no. 7, pp. 31–40.

Marcus, John. "Mining for Full-Text Gold on a Deadline: Information Technology Subject Coverage on the Three Major Services." *Database*, vol. 18, no. 2, April/May 1995, pp. 81–5.

McCarthy, Cheryl, Sylvia C. Krausse, and Arthur A. Little. "Expectations and Effectiveness Using CD-ROMS: What Do Patrons Want and How Satisfied are They?" *College & Research Libraries*, vol. 58, no. 2, March 1997, pp. 128–42.

McFaul, E. J. "CD-ROM Consistent Interface Guidelines: A Final Report." *CD-ROM Librarian*, vol. 7, no. 2, Feb. 1992, pp. 18–29.

McMillan, W. W. "Computing for Users with Special Needs and Models of Computer-Human Interaction." *CHI '92 Proceedings*, New York: Association for Computing Machinery, 1992, pp. 143–8.

"Microsoft 97." *Microsoft Office User Research Report*, Microsoft Corporation, 1997, pp. 1–8.

Miller, G. A. "The Magical Number Seven Plus or Minus Two: Some Limits on Our Capacity for Processing Information." *Psychological Review*, vol. 63, 1956, pp. 81–97.

Morkes, John, and Jakob Nielsen. "Applying Writing Guidelines to Web Pages." *CHI 98 Summary*, New York: Association for Computing Machinery, ACM Press, 1998, pp. 321–2.

Morris, M. E., and R. J. Hinrichs. *Web Page Design: A Different Multimedia.* Upper Saddle, N.J.: Prentice Hall, 1996.

Mountford, S. Joy, and W. Gaver. "Talking and Listening to Computers." In Brenda Laurel, ed. *The Art of Human-Computer Interface Design.* Reading, Mass.: Addison-Wesley Publishing Company, 1990, pp. 319–44.

Murdock, L., and O. Opello, "Computer Searches in the Physical Sciences," *Special Libraries*, vol. 64, no. 10, 1973, pp. 442–5.

Nardi, Bonnie. "Studying Context: A Comparison of Activity Theory, Situated Action Models, and Distributed Cognition." In *Context and Consciousness: Activity Theory and Human-Computer Interaction.* Cambridge, Mass.: MIT Press, 1995, pp. 69–102.

Nash, Stanley D., and Myoung C. Wilson. "Value-Added Bibliographic Instruction: Teaching Students to Find the Right Citations." *References Services Review*, 1991, vol. 19, no. 1, pp. 87–92.

Nicholls, Paul, and Jacqueline Ridley. "Evaluating Multimedia Library Materials: Clues from Hand-Printed Books and Art History." *Computers in Libraries*, April 1997, pp. 28–31.

Nicholls, Paul. "A Short Ride in a Fast Machine: CD-ROM Chronology." *CD-ROM Professional*, Nov. 1990, pp. 101–2.

Nielsen, Jakob, ed. *Advances in Human Computer Interaction*, vol. 5. Norwood, N.J.: Ablex Publishing, 1995.

———. *Designing Web Sites with Authority: Secrets of an Information Architect.* New York: New Riders Publishing, 1998.

———. "Is the Web Really Different from Everything Else?" *CHI 98: Human Factors in Computing Systems*, CHI 98 Summary, New York: Association for Computing Machinery, ACM Press, 1998, pp. 92–3.

———. *Multimedia and Hypertext: The Internet and Beyond.* Boston: AP Professional, 1995.

————. *Usability Engineering*. Boston: Academic Press, 1993.

————. "Usability Testing of WWW Designs." Sun Microsystems Web site. Available http://www.sun.com/sun-on-net/uidesign/usabilitytest.html. 21 Feb. 1999.

————. "User Interface Design for the WWW." Available http://www.acm.org/sigchi/chi97/proceedings/tutorial/jn.htm. 21 Feb. 1999.

Norman, Donald. *The Design of Everyday Things*. New York: Basic Books, 1990 (first released as *The Psychology of Everyday Things*, 1988).

————. *The Invisible Computer: Why Good Products Fail, the Personal Computer Is So Complex and Information Appliances Are the Solution*. Boston: MIT Press, 1998.

O'Connell, Pamela Licalzi. "Black Hole of E-Mail: Web Messages Like 2nd-Class Communication." *New York Times* story as it appeared in *The Santa Rosa Press Democrat*, July 10, 1998, p. E1.

O'Leary, Mick. "Dialog Tackles Retrieval in the Information Age." *ONLINE*, vol. 22, no. 3, May 1998, 57–64.

————. "The Business Information Services: Old Line Moves to the Web." *Computers in Libraries*, vol. 17, no. 6, June 1997, pp. 30–4.

Omanson, Richard C., Gavin S. Lew, and Robert M. Schumacher. "Creating Content for Both Paper and the Web." (Readability studies cited: Gould and Grischkowsky, 1984; Muter, Latremouille, Treurniet, and Beam, 1982; and Wright and Likorish, 1983), in Chris Forsythe, Eric Grose, and Julie Ratner, eds., *Human Factors and Web Development*, Mahwah, N.J.: Lawrence Erlbaum Publishers, 1998, pp. 199–206.

Paciello, Mike, and Yuri Rubinsky. "Making the Web Accessible for the Deaf, Hearing, and Mobility Impaired." 1996. Available http://www.samizdat. com/pac2.html. 21 Feb. 1999.

Parker, E., and W. J. Paisley. *Patterns of Information Seeking*. Stanford, Calif.: Stanford University Press, 1966.

Percival, J. Mark. "Graphic Interfaces and Online Information." *ONLINE Review*, vol. 14, no. 1, 1990, pp. 15–20.

Perritt, H. H. *The American with Disabilities Act Handbook*. 2nd. ed., New York: John Wiley and Sons, 1991.

Pitkow, J., and C. Kehoe, *GVU's 4th World-Wide Web User Survey*. Georgia Institute of Technology Web site. Available http://www.cc.gatech.edu/gvu/user_surveys/survey-10-1995/. 21 Feb. 1999.

————. *GVU's 6th World-Wide Web User Survey*. Georgia Institute of Technology Web site. Available http://www.cc.gatech.edu/gvu/user_surveys/survey-10-1996/. 21 Feb. 1999.

Polson, P. "The Consequences of Consistent and Inconsistent User Interfaces." In R. Guinden, ed., *Cognitive Science and Its Applications for Human-Computer Interaction.* Hillsdale, New Jersey: Erlbaum, 1988, pp. 59–89.

Powell, James E. *Designing User Interfaces.* San Marcos, Calif.: Microtrend, 1990, pp. 16–7.

Preece, Jenny, Yvonne Rogers, Helen Sharp, David Benyon, Simon Holland, and Tom Carey. *Human-Computer Interaction.* Harlow, England: Addison-Wesley Publishing Company, 1994.

Puttapithakporn, Somporn. "Interface Design and User Problems and Errors: A Case Study of Novice Searchers." *RQ*, vol. 30, no. 2, Winter 1990, pp. 195–204.

Rehkop, Barbara L. "Cypress: A GUI Interface to Dow Jones News/Retrieval." *ONLINE*, vol. 18, no. 1, Jan. 1994, pp. 72–5.

"Reviewer's Guide." *Microsoft Office 97*, Microsoft Corporation, Jan. 1997.

Rheinfrank, John, and Shelley Evenson. "Design Languages." In Terry Winograd with John Bennett, Laura DeYoung, and Bradley Hartfield, eds., *Bringing Design to Software*, Reading, Mass.: Addison-Wesley Publishing Company, 1996, pp. 63–80.

Richards, Trevor. "A Comparative Evaluation of Four Leading CD-ROM Retrieval Software Packages." *Computers in Libraries*, April 1995, pp. 70–5.

Richards, Trevor, and Christine Robinson. "Evaluating CD-ROM Software: A Model." *CD-ROM Professional*, Sept. 1993, pp. 96–101.

Rosenberg, John. "Road-Testing LEXIS-NEXIS' New Search Aid Software." *Searcher*, vol. 5, no. 7, July/Aug. 1997, pp. 48–58.

Rosenfeld, Louis, and Peter Morville. *Information Architecture for the World Wide Web.* Sebastopol, Calif.: O'Reilly, 1998.

Rothenberg, David. "How the Web Destroys the Quality of Students' Research Papers." *Chronicle of Higher Education*, August 15, 1997, p. A44.

Rowley, Jennifer, and Frances Slack. "The Evaluation of Interface Design on CDROMs." *Online and CDROM Review*, vol. 21, no. 1, 1997. pp. 3–13.

Rowley, Jennifer. "Human/Computer Interface Design in Windows-Based CD-ROMs: An Early Review." *Journal of Librarianship and Information Science*, vol. 27, no. 2, June 1995, pp. 77–87.

Salomon, Gitta. "New Uses of Color." In Brenda Laurel, ed. *The Art of Human-Computer Interface Design*, Reading, Mass.: Addison-Wesley Publishing Company, 1990, pp. 269–78.

Sandberg, Jared. "Dull Data Sites Become Shining Stars of the Web." *Wall Street Journal* article as it appeared in *The Santa Rosa Press Democrat*, July 26, 1998, p. E1.

Sanderson, Rosalie M. "The Continuing Saga of Professional End Users: Law Students Search Dialog at the University of Florida." *ONLINE*, vol. 14, no. 7, Nov., 1990, pp. 64–9.

Scoville, Richard. "Office Assistant: Dog or Genius?" Available http://www.pcworld.com/software/software_suites/articles/feb97/1502p106ff.html. 21 Feb. 1999.

Sellen, Abigail, and Nichol, Anne. "Building User-Centered On-line Help." In Brenda Laurel, ed. *The Art of Human-Computer Interface Design*, Reading, Mass.: Addison-Wesley Publishing Company, 1990, pp. 143–53.

Sevloid Guide to Web Design, Web site. Available http://www.sev.com.au/webzone/design.htm. 21 Feb. 1999.

Shaw, Debora. "The Human-Computer Interface for Information Retrieval." *Annual Review of Information Science and Technology*, vol. 26, 1991, pp. 155–95.

———. "Undergraduate Use of CD-ROM Databases: Observations of Human-Computer Interaction and Relevance Judgments." *Library and Information Science Research*, vol. 18, 1996, pp. 261–74.

Shenk, David. *Data Smog*. San Francisco: Harper Edge, 1997.

Shneiderman, Ben. "A Taxonomy and Rule Base for Selection of Interface Styles." In Ronald Baecker, Jonathan Grudin, William S. Buxton, and Saul Greenberg, eds., *Readings in Human-Computer Interaction: Toward the Year 2000*. San Francisco: Morgan Kaufman Publishers, Inc., 2nd ed., 1995, pp. 401–9.

———. *Designing the User Interface: Strategies for Effective Human-Computer Interaction*. Reading, Mass.: Addison-Wesley Publishing Company, 1993.

———. "Is the Web Really Different from Everything Else?" *CHI 98: Human Factors in Computing Systems Summary*, New York: Association for Computing Machinery, ACM Press, 1998, p. 92.

Shubin, Hal, and Ron Perkins. "Web Navigation: Resolving Conflicts Between the Desktop and the Web." *CHI 98 Summary*, ACM Conference Proceedings, New York: Association for Computing Machinery, 1998, p. 209.

Siegel, David. *Creating Killer Web Sites*, Indianapolis: Hayden Books, 1996.

———. *Secrets of Successful Web Sites: Project Management on the World Wide Web*. Indianapolis: Hayden Books, 1997.

Spool, Jared M., Tara Scanlon, Will Schroeder, Carolyn Snyder, and Terri DeAngelo. *Web Usability: A Designer's Guide*. Andover, Mass.: User Interface Engineering, 1997.

Spool, Jared. "Surprises on the Web," *User Interface Engineering Web Site*. Oct. 1996. Available http://world.std.com/~uieweb/surprise.htm. 21 Feb. 1999.

Summerfield, Mary; Carol A. Mandel; and Paul Kantor. "Online Books at Columbia: Measurement and Early Results on Use, Satisfaction, and Effect." *Scholarly*

Communication and Technology Conference by the Andrew Mellon Foundation, July 1997. Available http://arl.cni.org/scomm/scat/summerfield.ind.com. 21 Feb. 1999.

Sun Microsystems' Enabling Technologies Web Page. Web site available http://www.sun.com/tech/access/acess.quick.ref.html. 21 Feb. 1999.

Sun's Guide to Web Style. Available http://www.sun.com/styleguide/. 21 Feb. 1999.

Sutton, Stuart A. "Core Competencies for the Information Professions and the Evolution of Skills Sets." *Education Libraries,* vol. 18, no. 3, pp. 6–11.

Tauscher, Linda, and Saul Greenberg, "Revisitation Patterns in World Wide Web Navigation," *CHI 97 Proceedings,* ACM Conference Proceedings, New York: Association for Computing Machinery, 1997, pp. 399–406.

"Tremble Everyone." *The Economist,* May 10, 1997, pp. E10–E13.

Tufte, Edward. *Envisioning Information.* Cheshire, Conn.: Graphics Press, 1990.

"Usability Testing of World Wide Web Sites." *SIGCHI WWW SIA: CHI 97.* Available http://www.acm.org/sigchi/web/chi97testing/ricknote.htm. 21 Feb. 1999.

Vanderheiden, G. C. "Thirty-Something Million: Should They Be Exceptions?" *Human Factors,* vol. 32, no. 4, 1990, pp. 383–96.

Verplank, William. "Graphic Challenges in Designing Object-Oriented User Interfaces." In M. Helander, ed., *Handbook of Human-Computer Interaction.* New York: North Holland, 1988, pp. 365–76.

Vickery, Brian, and Alina Vickery. "Online Search Interface Design." *The Journal of Documentation,* vol. 49, no. 2, June 1993, pp. 103–87.

Weber, Thomas. "E-Mail Queries Confound Companies." *The Wall Street Journal* article as it appeared in *The Santa Rosa Press Democrat,* Oct. 28, 1996, p. E1.

Weibe, Eric N., and Julie E. Howe. "Graphics Design on the Web." In Chris Forsythe, Eric Grose, and Julie Ratner, eds. *Human Factors and Web Development,* Mahwah, N.J.: Lawrence Erlbaum Publishers, 1998, pp. 225–39.

Wickens, Charles. "Attention in Perception and Display Space." *Engineering Psychology and Human Performance,* Boston: Little-Brown, 1992, pp. 74–115.

Winograd, Terry, with John Bennett, Laura DeYoung, and Bradley Hartfield, eds. *Bringing Design to Software.* Reading, Mass.: Addison-Wesley Publishing Company, 1996.

Wooliams, Peter, and David Gee. "Accounting for User Diversity in Configuring Online Systems." *ONLINE Review,* vol. 16, no. 5, 1992, pp. 303–11.

"XML Packages Data Like an Envelope." *Web 98 Conference,* Sept. 23, 1998. Available http://webreview.com/wr/pub/web98east/23/xmlday2.html. 21 Feb. 1999.

Zimmerman, Beverly B. "Applying Tufte's Principles of Information Design to Creating Effective Web Pages." *SIGDOC 97*, Snowbird, Utah, 1997. ACM Conference Proceedings, New York: Association for Computing Machinery, 1997, pp. 309–17.

Zink, Stephen. "Toward More Critical Reviewing and Analysis of CD-ROM User Software Interfaces." *CD-ROM Professional*, vol. 4, no. 1, January 1991, pp. 16–22.

Note: Date following Web citations indicates date of access.

Index

About the Author

Alison J. Head is an information management consultant, lecturer, and writer. She works on Web and intranet design projects, conducting usability testing and design analyses for Hewlett-Packard and other information-intensive companies. Alison is the former Director of Information Management at *The Press Democrat Newspaper*, a New York Times Regional Newspaper in Santa Rosa, California. She has taught in the Graduate School of Library and Information Science at San Jose State University and in the Communication Department at Saint Mary's College of California. Alison is a regular contributor to *ONLINE* magazine and Planet-IT (http://www.planetit.com).

Alison has a Ph.D. in Library and Information Science from the University of California at Berkeley and was recently a Visiting Scholar at Stanford University, where she studied Human-Computer Interaction.

Alison lives in Sonoma, California, with her husband, Mark Pollock, and her dog, Madeline.

More CyberAge Books from Information Today, Inc.

Electronic Styles
A Handbook for Citing Electronic Information
Xia Li and Nancy Crane
The second edition of the best-selling guide to referencing electronic information and citing the complete range of electronic formats includes text-based information, electronic journals and discussion lists, Web sites, CD-ROM and multimedia products, and commercial online documents.
Softbound • ISBN 1-57387-027-7 • $19.99

Secrets of the Super Net Searchers
Reva Basch • Foreword by Howard Rheingold
Reva Basch, top online searcher and cyber-journalist, reveals the insights, anecdotes, tips, techniques, and case studies of 35 of the world's top Internet hunters and gatherers. These Super Net Searchers explain how to find valuable information on the Internet, including where the Internet shines as a research tool, distinguishing cyber-gems from cyber-junk, and how to avoid "Internet Overload."
Softbound • ISBN 0-910965-22-6 • $29.95

Finding Statistics Online
How to Locate the Elusive Numbers You Need
Paula Berinstein • Edited by Susanne Bjørner
Need statistics? Find them more quickly and easily than ever–online! Finding good statistics is a challenge for even the most experienced researcher. Today, it's likely the statistics you need are available online–but where? This book explains how to effectively use the Internet and professional online systems to find the statistics you need to succeed.
Softbound • ISBN 0-910965-25-0 • $29.95

The Extreme Searcher's Guide to Web Search Engines
A Handbook for the Serious Searcher
Randolph Hock • Foreword by Paula Berinstein
Whether you're a new Web user or an experienced online searcher, here's a practical guide that shows you how to make the most of the leading Internet search tools. Written by leading Internet trainer Randolph (Ran) Hock, this book gives an in-depth view of the major search engines, explaining their respective strengths and weaknesses, features, and providing detailed instructions on how to use each to its maximum potential. As a reader bonus the author is maintaining a regularly updated directory online.
Softbound • ISBN 0-910965-26-9 • $24.95
Hardbound • ISBN 0-910965-38-2 • $34.95

Great Scouts!
CyberGuides to Subject Searching on the Web
Nora Paul and Margot Williams
Edited by Paula Hane • Foreword by Barbara Quint

Great Scouts! is a cure for information overload. Authors Nora Paul (The Poynter Institute) and Margot Williams *(The Washington Post)* direct readers to the very best subject-specific, Web-based information resources. Thirty chapters cover specialized "CyberGuides" selected as the premier Internet sources of information on business, education, arts and entertainment, science and technology, health and medicine, politics and government, law, sports, and much more. With its expert advice and evaluations of information and link content, value, currency, stability, and usability, *Great Scouts!* takes you "beyond search engines"—and directly to the top sources of information for your topic.

Softbound • ISBN 0-910965-27-7 • $24.95

Super Searchers Do Business
The Online Secrets of Top Business Researchers
Mary Ellen Bates • Edited by Reva Basch

Super Searchers Do Business probes the minds of 11 leading researchers who use the Internet and online services to find critical business information. Through her in-depth interviews, Mary Ellen Bates—a business super searcher herself—gets the pros to reveal how they choose online sources, evaluate search results, and tackle the most challenging business research projects. Loaded with expert tips, techniques, and strategies, this is the first title in the exciting new "Super Searchers" series, edited by Reva Basch. If you do business research online, or plan to, let *Super Searchers Do Business* be your guide.

Softbound • ISBN 0-910965-33-1 • $24.95

Naked in Cyberspace
How to Find Personal Information Online
Carole A. Lane • Foreword by Helen Burwell

Now that so many types of personal records are searchable online, the bureaucratic red tape that used to protect our secrets from prying eyes has been stripped away...and we're all naked in cyberspace. Without taking sides on the right and wrong of using online ingredients to compile a detailed dossier, *Naked in Cyberspace* tells you where to find personal information online and on CD-ROM.

Softbound • ISBN 0-910965-17-X • $29.95
